JAY-Z

Building a Hip-Hop Empire

By Vanessa Oswald

Portions of this book originally appeared in *Jay-Z* by Laurie Collier Hillstrom.

Published in 2019 by
Lucent Press, an Imprint of Greenhaven Publishing, LLC
353 3rd Avenue
Suite 255
New York, NY 10010

Designer: Deanna Paternostro
Editor: Vanessa Oswald

Library of Congress Cataloging-in-Publication Data

Names: Oswald, Vanessa, author.
Title: Jay-Z : building a hip-hop empire / Vanessa Oswald.
Description: New York : Lucent Press, [2019] | Series: People in the news |
    Includes bibliographical references and index.
Identifiers: LCCN 2018001693 (print) | LCCN 2018002438 (ebook) | ISBN
    9781534563360 (eBook) | ISBN 9781534563353 (library bound book) | ISBN
    9781534563377 (pbk. book)
Subjects: LCSH: Jay-Z, 1969–Juvenile literature. | Rap musicians–United
    States–Biography–Juvenile literature.
Classification: LCC ML3930.J38 (ebook) | LCC ML3930.J38 O79 2019 (print) |
    DDC 782.421649092 [B] –dc23
LC record available at https://lccn.loc.gov/2018001693

Printed in the United States of America

CPSIA compliance information: Batch #BS18KL: For further information contact Greenhaven Publishing LLC, New York,
New York at 1-844-317-7404.

Please visit our website, www.greenhavenpublishing.com. For a free color
catalog of all our high-quality books, call toll free 1-844-317-7404 or
fax 1-844-317-7405.

Contents

Foreword

We live in a world where the latest news is always available and where it seems we have unlimited access to the lives of the people in the news. Entire television networks are devoted to news about politics, sports, and entertainment. Social media has allowed people to have an unprecedented level of interaction with celebrities. We have more information at our fingertips than ever before. However, how much do we really know about the people we see on television news programs, social media feeds, and magazine covers?

Despite the constant stream of news, the full stories behind the lives of some of the world's most newsworthy men and women are often unknown. Who was Katy Perry before she was a pop music phenomenon? What does LeBron James do when he's not playing basketball? What inspires Lin-Manuel Miranda?

This series aims to answer questions like these about some of the biggest names in pop culture, sports, politics, and technology. While the subjects of this series come from all walks of life and areas of expertise, they share a common magnetism that has made them all captivating figures in the public eye. They have shaped the world in some unique way, and—in many cases—they are poised to continue to shape the world for many years to come.

These biographies are not just a collection of basic facts. They tell compelling stories that show how each figure grew to become a powerful public personality. Each book aims to paint a complete, realistic picture of its subject—from the challenges they overcame to the controversies they caused. In doing so, each book reinforces the idea that even the most famous faces on the news are real people who are much more complex than we are often shown in brief video clips or sound bites. Readers are also reminded that there is even more to a person than what they present to the world through social media posts, press releases, and interviews. The whole story of a person's life can only be discovered by digging beneath the surface of their public persona, and that is what this series allows readers to do.

The books in this series are filled with enlightening quotes from speeches and interviews given by the subjects, as well as quotes and anecdotes from those who know their story best: family, friends, coaches, and colleagues. All quotes are noted to provide guidance for further research. Detailed lists of additional resources are also included, as are timelines, indexes, and unique photographs. These text features come together to enhance the reading experience and encourage readers to dive deeper into the stories of these influential men and women.

Fame can be fleeting, but the subjects featured in this series have real staying power. They have fundamentally impacted their respective fields and have achieved great success through hard work and true talent. They are men and women defined by their accomplishments, and they are often seen as role models for the next generation. They have left their mark on the world in a major way, and their stories are meant to inspire readers to leave their mark, too.

Introduction

Rise to the Top

S hawn Carter, known to the world as JAY-Z, is widely considered to be one of the most successful rap artists of all time. Like many rappers, he has had various stage names throughout the years, such as Jaÿ-Z, Jay-Z, JAY Z, and his current stage name of JAY-Z. He has sold more than 36 million records in the United States, dominated radio airplay, and won several Grammy Awards during the course of his career. "He spit cool and witty with devastating flows, dropped classic albums, influenced MCs, changed pop culture and built a tall stack of dollars in the process," noted a writer for *Rolling Stone* magazine. "We've witnessed not merely a Hall of Fame career but one of the top-shelf greatest of all time."[1]

Boss of Business

While JAY-Z is well-known for his rap career, his legacy extends far beyond the music he has created. He also built his own business empire—including an influential record label and a popular clothing line—and ascended to one of the most powerful positions in the music industry as president and chief executive officer (CEO) of Def Jam Records. His rise to the top is all the more remarkable considering where he started. "I've taken the whole ride," he acknowledged. "I didn't skip any floors. I started at the

JAY-Z is not only a rapper; he is also a businessman and devoted son and father.

lower lobby. Went all the way up to the penthouse."[2]

JAY-Z grew up poor in a tough New York City neighborhood. After being abandoned by his father, he became a drug dealer in his teens. However, JAY-Z eventually escaped the hard life of a street hustler through talent, determination, and ambition. He stands as an example "of what anyone—no matter their class, economic level, race, environment, social status, or adversities—can achieve with hard work and hustle,"[3] Jake Brown wrote in *JAY-Z ... and the Roc-A-Fella Records Dynasty*. "JAY-Z is a fundamental example of the hip-hop renaissance man, and a pioneer of the model—street hustler to rap star to rap mogul in his own right."[4]

By combining musical talent, business know-how, and street smarts, JAY-Z has emerged as one of the most influential figures in American music and hip-hop culture. His success story serves as an inspiration to his many fans. "Jay-Z's trailblazing contributions to hip-hop culture across America and throughout the world have helped raise the aspirations of millions of people," Def Jam Records co-founder Russell Simmons wrote. "He has had the courage to tell vivid stories about the realities of the urban experience with the precision of a master therapist whose words and rhymes tap into the consciousness of people who yearn for a better life ... Today JAY-Z stands center stage with the penetrating sustainability of a living legend."[5]

Family Man

Living in the fast lane with his music career, JAY-Z makes sure to slow down occasionally to spend quality time with his family. He is married to the equally successful recording artist Beyoncé Knowles, with whom he has three children: daughter Blue Ivy, daughter Rumi, and Rumi's twin brother Sir. The family has taken many trips together to destinations such as the Grand Canyon, Hawai'i, and Italy.

JAY-Z shares his empire with his wife, Beyoncé, and children Blue Ivy (shown here), Rumi, and Sir.

Throughout their relationship, JAY-Z and Beyoncé have made an intense effort to keep much of their personal life out of the spotlight; however, several private details of the family's life have become public due to the media's coverage. Despite the drama-filled reports plastered on numerous tabloid magazines and websites, the family had stated that their bond is strong. The couple has run into their fair share of disputes, such as cheating allegations and lawsuits, but have faced these challenges head on, expressing and resolving these issues in their own unique ways—one of them, sometimes, being through their music.

As JAY-Z has done with most obstacles in his life, he has risen to the occasion in the face of adversity. Through his many talents as a recording artist and a businessman he has built a life he can be proud of, but also he does not claim to have it all figured out. He has admitted defeat in the past and strives to break through his own personal barriers with each day that passes to continue to become a better rapper, husband, and father.

Chapter **One**

Finding His Way

JAY-Z's upbringing as a young boy helped shape the multidimensional artist he is today. Part of his enormous appeal in the world of hip-hop comes from his "street cred." When he raps about poverty, crime, drugs, and violence, he speaks from his past experiences. JAY-Z grew up in a tough urban neighborhood and got a firsthand look at life as a drug dealer. However, he used music to lift himself out of this cruel and self-destructive existence. His remarkable rise from the streets of the ghetto to the top of the recording industry helped him earn the respect and admiration of millions of fans.

Living in the Marcy Projects

Shawn Corey Carter was born on December 4, 1969, in Brooklyn, one of the five boroughs that comprise New York City. His mother, Gloria Carter, worked as an investment analyst and his father, Adnis Reeves, held a series of odd jobs. "My pops did anything from cabdriver to truck driver to working at the phone company,"[6] he recalled. Shawn was the youngest of four children in his family. He had one older brother, Eric, and two older sisters, Andrea (known as Annie) and Michelle (known as Mickey).

JAY-Z grew up in the Marcy Houses, a large public housing

The Marcy Houses were known for their drugs and crime.

complex for low-income families, located in the Bedford-Stuyvesant neighborhood of Brooklyn. Built in 1949, Marcy consisted of 27 different 6-story apartment buildings that housed more than 4,000 people. It was a tough place to grow up and was full of drugs and crime. CBS News once described the Marcy Houses as "among the most dangerous places in America."[7] Looking back, though, JAY-Z noted that his background gave him a valuable perspective on life:

I wouldn't want to grow up no other way. It shaped me, taught me integrity ... You've got kids that inherited stuff from their parents [and] They don't appreciate it because it was no work; there's no A to Z, it's just Z. To me, you need somewhere to start, somewhere to be like, 'Man, I ain't never going back to not being able to pay my light bill, my stomach growling, eating cereal at night, peanut butter and jelly off the spoon, mayonnaise sandwiches.' This is real.[8]

Despite the hardships that he suffered, JAY-Z managed to keep a positive attitude. Even as a boy, he was a bit of a showoff and enjoyed being the center of attention. His friends and neighbors gave him the nickname "Jazzy," which he eventually shortened to create the first version of his stage name, Jay-Z. "When I *was* young I had the same demeanor as I do now. I was a cool kid, a jazzy little dude. People would say, 'Yo, it's Jazzy!'" he explained. "I liked the way it flowed so I took the Jay and the Z."[9] He also adopted this name as homage to his mentor Jaz-O.

Evolution of a Stage Name

Several rappers and performers with stage names sometimes alter their names to match the specific personas they embody at different times throughout their careers. One example of an artist who has done this is Snoop Dogg, whose real name is Calvin Cordozar Broadus Jr. His stage names include Snoop Doggy Dogg, Snoop Lion, Snoopzilla, DJ Snoopadelic, and Snoop Rock. Another rapper who has changed his stage name multiple times is Diddy, whose real name is Sean Combs. In the past he has also gone by Puffy, P. Diddy, and Puff Daddy.

As a young kid, Shawn Carter was known in his neighborhood as "Jazzy," which evolved into his original stage name Jay-Z, which he created in the late 1980s. As his career as a rapper grew, he decided to remove the hyphen in 2013. He explained the reasoning behind his decision: "The hyphen was really big back in the day. It's not useful anymore ... I had umlauts over one of the letters; I removed that too."[1] Over the years Carter has gone by the names Jay-Z, Jaÿ-Z, and JAY Z. In 2017, he reintroduced the hyphen to his name while keeping it stylized in all capital letters to form JAY-Z. Additional nicknames he has been given include Young Hov, J-Hova, Hova, Jigga, and Jiggaman.

1. Quoted in Nerisha Penrose, "JAY-Z & More Rappers Who Have Changed Their Names Over the Years," *Billboard*, June 20, 2017. www.billboard.com/articles/columns/hip-hop/7840929/jay-z-rapper-name-changes-hyphen.

Music Lover

Even as a boy, Shawn's love for music was abundant. His parents had many albums that they had collected over the years. Each album had a label with the owner's name on it, and no one else in the family was allowed to touch it without permission. "These people shared everything," JAY-Z remembered about his parents, "but not (our) records. It was like, 'This is my son and your son. This is my house and your house. But this is my record.' That's just to show you how much they loved their music."[10]

Gloria Carter always listened to music on Saturdays while she cleaned the family's apartment. Even when he was outdoors, JAY-Z could hear his mother's soul and funk records blaring through the open windows. He loved the rhythm of the music, but he often found himself making up different words to match the beat. He spent hours at the kitchen table playing with words, coming up with inventive rhymes, and experimenting with song lyrics. "I had this green notebook that I used to write in incessantly," he recalled. "I would walk through the Marcy projects, where everyone's playing basketball, with my notebook, and that was not a cool thing."[11]

If young Shawn did not have his notebook handy, he wrote down lyrics on scraps of paper or grocery sacks and stuffed them into his pockets. When all these scraps of paper became annoying, he developed the ability to compose entire songs in his head without writing them down. "I started running around in the streets, and that's how not writing came about," he explained. "I was comin' up with these ideas, and I'd write 'em on a paper bag, and I had all these paper bags in my pocket, and I hate a lot of things in my pocket, so I started memorizing and holding it."[12]

When a Father Leaves

As Shawn approached his teen years, he dreamed of pursuing a career in music. He needed this dream to sustain him when his family was suddenly torn apart. In 1981, when Shawn was 11, his father left home. Adnis Reeves divorced his wife and had no further contact with his children, leaving Shawn devastated. "Kids look up to they pop like Superman. Superman just left the crib? That's traumatic," he acknowledged. "He was a good guy. It's just that he didn't handle the situation well. He handled it so bad that you forgot all the good this guy did."[13]

Shawn struggled to deal with feelings of pain, anger, confusion, and resentment after his father left the family. He developed a fear of abandonment that made it difficult for him to establish close relationships with other people. "I changed a lot. I became more guarded," he said. "I never wanted to be attached to something and get that taken away again. I never wanted to feel that feeling again."[14]

Shawn's mother worried about him and did her best to keep him out of trouble. She bought him his own boom box to encourage his interest in music. Despite her best efforts, though, the family went through some tough times. Money was tight, and they often struggled to pay the electric bill or put food on the table. Shawn's brother, Eric, started doing drugs and became addicted. One day, when Shawn was 12, he caught Eric stealing jewelry that belonged to him. Eric planned to sell it for money to buy drugs. Angry and disappointed, Shawn got a gun from someone on the street and shot his older brother in the shoulder. Luckily, Eric recovered from the wound and forgave him, and Shawn did not face criminal charges.

Life on the Streets

As he watched his family struggle in the absence of his father, Shawn found it hard to resist the temptations he saw around him on the street. Many people in the projects, like his brother, turned to drugs as a way to escape from their problems. Other people—including kids his own age—made money by selling drugs. The drug of choice in his neighborhood at that time was crack cocaine. It was very popular among poor drug users because it was cheaper than regular cocaine but produced an intense high. Crack use spread through large American cities like an epidemic in the mid-1980s, contributing to existing problems such as homelessness, poverty, and crime. The crack epidemic hit the Marcy Houses hard. "It was a plague in that neighborhood," JAY-Z remembered. "It was just everywhere, everywhere you look. In the hallways. You could smell it in the hallways."[15]

In the midst of the crack epidemic, Shawn felt that he had two choices: do drugs or sell drugs. "It was either you're doin' it or you was movin' it,"[16] he stated. After witnessing the effects of his brother's addiction, he was determined not to do drugs. However, the lure of easy money was very powerful, so he started working as a drug dealer. He sold crack cocaine in his Brooklyn neighborhood, gradually expanding his territory into New Jersey. The money he earned enabled him to buy nice clothes and jewelry. He also gave some to his mother to help his family live more comfortably.

Although he needed the money, he knew that selling illegal drugs exposed him to a great deal of risk. He had to watch his

A Gifted Student

Before he dropped out of high school to pursue a career in music, JAY-Z was a very good student. By the time he reached sixth grade, he was already reading at a twelfth-grade level. In addition, his remarkable memory—which he used to compose entire songs in his head—helped him perform well on tests.

JAY-Z's favorite teacher was Renee Rosenblum-Lowden, who taught his English class in middle school. "She took our class to her house in Brooklyn on a field trip," he recalled. "You know how many teachers would take a bunch of black kids to their house?"[1] His teacher remembered him as a sweet, good-natured young man with a gift for language. "He was a very dear kid," Rosenblum-Lowden said. "There is so much more to him than a [stereotypical rapper]."[2]

1. Quoted in Mitchell Fink, "Rapper Jay-Z Waxes Lyrical About Teacher," *New York Daily News*, February 16, 1999. www.nydailynews.com/archives/gossip/rapper-jay-z-waxes-lyrical-teacher-article-1.824397.

2. Quoted in Nick Charles and Cynthia Wang, "Street Singer," *People*, April 5, 1999. people.com/archive/street-singer-vol-51-no-12/.

back all the time to avoid getting caught by the police. He felt nervous anytime he saw a police car in his rearview mirror. He also had to be careful to avoid confrontations with other drug dealers. He knew that many people in his line of work became victims of violence. JAY-Z said, "I knew I had to get out [of the drug business] because the only future is jail or die."[17]

Musical Career Beginnings

Even as he continued to hustle drugs on the street, Shawn also worked toward building a brighter future for himself. He went to school and got good grades. He attended Eli Whitney High School in his neighborhood until it closed down, then qualified for admission to Brooklyn's prestigious George Westinghouse Career and Technical Education High School. It was there that he met several fellow students who shared his interest in music, including Christopher Wallace (who later became known as The Notorious B.I.G.).

Shawn and his friends were intrigued by hip-hop, a relatively new form of music that gained widespread popularity in the mid-1980s. Hip-hop originated in New York City during the 1970s, when a Jamaican-American disc jockey (DJ) named Kool Herc began reciting his own rhymes over the background beat of recorded music. Before long, kids throughout the city were going to house parties where DJs used multiple turntables to mix parts of popular records together to create new songs. Talented masters of ceremonies (MCs) rapped rhyming lyrics to the music, while people in the crowd performed break dancing moves. By the middle of the 1980s, hip-hop songs by groups such as Run-DMC and the Beastie Boys had started to receive some radio airplay.

Shawn practiced rapping constantly, in hopes of becoming part of this exciting new music scene. "For years every morning he'd wake up and be in the mirror rhyming to hisself, to hear himself and see how he's pronouncing words and checkin' his flow," his cousin Briant "Bee-High" Biggs remembered. "Every morning. You know how some people get up and do they calisthenics [exercises] every morning? That was his thing."[18] Sometimes

Shawn and his friends performed on street corners or at parties. He eventually became known throughout his neighborhood as a talented rapper.

Shawn's growing reputation gave him opportunities to work with other up-and-coming hip-hop artists. When he was 18, he began performing with a fellow Marcy Houses resident known as Jaz-O or Big Jaz. When Jaz-O signed a contract to cut an album for the EMI record label in 1989, he asked Shawn to appear on it. Shawn rapped on the song "Hawaiian Sophie," which was played on the radio in New York City and became a minor hit. He also rapped on the 1994 song "Show and Prove" by Brooklyn recording artist Big Daddy Kane.

Rap Focus

With each successful collaboration, the rapper we know today as JAY-Z continued to build a following among the city's hip-hop fans and expand his contacts in the music business. Many people he met were impressed by his willingness to work hard to improve upon his natural abilities. "He was ambitious and he wanted to get better every day," recalled DJ and record producer Clark Kent. "And it's funny how effortlessly it came to him. He's just gifted."[19]

As his music career showed signs of blossoming, he lost interest in both selling drugs and doing schoolwork. He decided to drop out of high school and quit selling drugs to focus on his dream of becoming a recording artist. Although it was hard to give up the money that selling drugs provided, Shawn was tired of worrying about getting killed or thrown in prison. He got a legitimate job and started saving money to record his own album.

After working for several years, he finally earned enough to pay for sessions in a recording studio. He recorded his first original song, "In My Lifetime," and had it turned into a single. The lyrics told a gritty, realistic story about growing up in the projects and working as a drug dealer. Shawn Carter—now known as Jay-Z—worked hard to promote the song. In the early 1990s, he sold copies from the trunk of his car in the streets of Brooklyn. He also took copies into radio stations and nightclubs and convinced

DJs to play it.

In the meantime, JAY-Z continued recording songs with the hope of putting together an entire album. His work attracted the attention of a couple of record labels that offered to help him produce and promote the album. JAY-Z knew that signing a contract with a label would allow him to rent a top recording studio and give his album widespread distribution. However, he also knew that powerful record companies sometimes took advantage of promising young

Jaz-O (shown here) was one of JAY-Z's first mentors.

artists. They often limited new artists' creative control by insisting that they work with established record producers. They also typically took a large chunk of the profits from album sales in exchange for arranging concert tours, making videos, and other promotional activities. JAY-Z understood the pitfalls of the music business from watching friends such as Jaz-O release successful albums without earning much money. He decided to take a risk and try a different approach.

Roc-A-Fella Records

Rather than sign a contract with a big record label, JAY-Z decided to form his own label. Along with two partners, Damon "Dame" Dash and Kareem "Biggs" Burke, he launched Roc-A-Fella Records in 1995. It was one of a growing number of independent record labels that were formed around that time.

Damon Dash (left), JAY-Z, and Kareem Burke (right) came together to start Roc-A-Fella Records in 1995.

Dash had gained experience in the music industry as a promoter, so he handled the day-to-day business operations at Roc-A-Fella. Burke had a talent for tracking the latest news on the street, so he worked to keep the label at the forefront of hip-hop trends and styles. The first step in building Roc-A-Fella into a successful business, however, involved releasing JAY-Z's debut album. To guarantee that the record would get into stores, the partners ultimately signed a distribution deal with Priority Records. Priority produced the album and handled distribution, but JAY-Z retained full creative control.

Reasonable Doubt

The result of his hard work, *Reasonable Doubt*, was released in June 1996. It featured 15 tracks that provided a highly personal account of his experiences as a drug dealer. JAY-Z rapped about the financial rewards of that life as well as the dangers. His realism and clever wordplay made the album an immediate hit. It earned gold record status within 3 months by selling more than 500,000 copies, and it climbed as high as number 23 on the Billboard 200 chart. The album eventually went on to earn platinum status with lifetime sales of more than 1 million copies.

In addition to the solid sales figures, *Reasonable Doubt* received high praise from music critics. AllMusic reviewer Steve Huey called it "an instant classic of a debut, detailing his experiences on the streets with disarming honesty, and writing some of the most acrobatic rhymes heard in quite some time."[20]

The first single from the album to appear on the Billboard charts was "Ain't No N***a (Like the One I Got)," which featured the female rapper Foxy Brown. Although JAY-Z's lyrics were playful and humorous and the song had a danceable beat, many people objected to the obscene language in the title. Some radio stations refused to play the song, while others edited the word out or replaced it with "brother" or "player." The controversy actually increased the song's popularity, and it remained at the top of the dance charts for five weeks. Other singles that received a lot of airplay included "Dead Presidents" and "Can't Knock the Hustle," which featured guest vocals by Mary J. Blige.

While JAY-Z appreciated the good reviews and sales figures for his first album, he was most gratified by the way his work seemed to connect with hip-hop fans. His songs held great meaning for some people, especially those who shared his experience of growing up in a tough urban neighborhood. "There were cats coming up to me like, 'You must have been looking in my window or following my life,'" he said. "It was emotional. Like big, rough hoodlum, hardrock, three-time jail bidders with scars and gold teeth just breaking down. It was something to look at, like, I must be going somewhere where people been wanting somebody to go for a while."[21]

Chapter **Two**

Moving Up the Rap Ladder

With the successful release of his first album, *Reasonable Doubt*, JAY-Z established himself as a promising new rap artist. He was determined to build upon this success and become a huge star. During the late 1990s—a time when the world of hip-hop music lost The Notorious B.I.G. and Tupac Shakur, two of its most influential figures, to violence—JAY-Z released a series of albums that sold millions of copies and earned multiple Grammy nominations. He also expanded his business interests to include clothing and films. Shortly before the decade ended, however, JAY-Z became entangled in a violent incident that placed his future in jeopardy.

Def Jam Deal

JAY-Z's successful debut album turned Roc-A-Fella Records into a major player in the rap music industry. The hit record gave the fledgling independent label instant credibility and visibility. Before long, both powerful record companies and up-and-coming rap artists were clamoring to work with Roc-A-Fella. JAY-Z and his partners took advantage of the opportunity to grow their business. In early 1997, they signed a joint venture agreement with Def Jam, the record company that had brought rap music to a large audience by promoting such early stars as Run-DMC and LL Cool J.

The deal put Def Jam in charge of promotion but ensured that Roc-A-Fella maintained creative control. The two companies also agreed to share ownership rights to all original or master recordings, meaning that they would each receive 50 percent of the profits from future uses of copyrighted songs. After finalizing the deal, Roc-A-Fella worked to find and promote new talent, such as Brooklyn rapper Memphis Bleek. The label also planned a three-volume series of albums by its premier artist, JAY-Z.

While JAY-Z was working on his second album, violence rocked the world of rap music. A high-profile feud between East Coast and West Coast rappers had spiraled to the point that two rap giants—Tupac Shakur and The Notorious B.I.G.—were shot and killed within a few months of each other. JAY-Z went to high school with The Notorious B.I.G. and worked with him on the song "Brooklyn's Finest," which had appeared on *Reasonable Doubt*. The death of his friend affected JAY-Z deeply. He wanted to honor The Notorious B.I.G.'s legacy by helping to heal the divisions in the rap world, while also hoping to claim The Notorious B.I.G.'s title as the greatest star on the East Coast scene.

To achieve these goals, JAY-Z worked with one of the best record producers in the business, Sean Combs (who has also been known as Puff Daddy, Puffy, P. Diddy, and Diddy). During their recording sessions, JAY-Z's ability to compose entire songs within minutes and commit them to memory astounded Combs. "He writes in his head. You'll hear grunts and 'Woo!'—like he's impressed by what he's writing," the producer recalled. "Of course you're watching; you feel a little left out, like, 'Let me hear what you're saying!' But he keeps writing, then he goes into a [recording] booth."[22]

The Follow-Up Album

JAY-Z released the result of his and Combs's collaboration, *In My*

East Coast versus West Coast

The reputation of rap music suffered greatly in the mid-1990s following several heavily publicized incidents of violence involving rappers from the East and West Coasts of the United States. The West Coast rappers, centered in Los Angeles, California, and under contract with Death Row Records, included Tupac Shakur, Snoop Dogg, and Dr. Dre. The East Coast rappers, centered in New York City and under contract with Bad Boy Records, were led by The Notorious B.I.G. and Sean Combs. Many of these artists released songs that featured violent lyrics and threats or insults aimed at their rivals across the country.

The most high-profile feud involved Tupac Shakur and The Notorious B.I.G. In 1994, Tupac was shot during a trip to New York and claimed that Bad Boy Records

Lifetime: Volume 1, on November 4, 1997. As the title suggests, the album featured a number of songs about JAY-Z's youth and early rap career. The album contained some hardcore rap songs, but most of the tracks had a more mainstream, pop-oriented sound than those on his first album. Some listeners complained that the lighter tone meant that JAY-Z was selling out his existing fans to reach a wider audience. They claimed that he had lost some of his street credibility in his attempt to create a crossover hit.

Some reviewers, however, praised JAY-Z for exploring more mature themes in *Volume 1*. They felt that he struck a good balance between respecting his roots and moving on to address other concerns. Several songs on the album focused on the challenges JAY-Z faced in his new life as a successful recording artist and owner of a record label. In the track "Lucky Me," for instance, he revealed some of the negative aspects of life as a famous rapper.

was responsible. The Notorious B.I.G. denied the charge and made fun of Tupac in his song "Who Shot Ya?" The following year, Tupac responded with "Hit 'Em Up," in which he insulted The Notorious B.I.G.'s wife, singer Faith Evans.

The feud culminated in the murder of Tupac in Las Vegas, Nevada, in September 1996, followed by the murder of The Notorious B.I.G. in March 1997 in Los Angeles. Both cases went unsolved. The deaths of the two prominent artists hit the rap world hard. Many people demanded an end to the violence and called on rappers to settle their disputes with words rather than guns.

The deaths of Tupac and The Notorious B.I.G. still affect the hip-hop world and remain a subject of interest for many. In 2018, USA Network debuted the fictionalized series *Unsolved: The Murders of Tupac and The Notorious B.I.G.*, which covers the deaths of the rappers and the attempts to solve the tragic crimes.

Even though he was wealthy and successful, he noted that he did not feel much safer being a rapper than when he had been a drug dealer. The violence swirling around the world of rap at the time had even convinced him to wear a bulletproof vest while on stage or at parties.

JAY-Z used another song on the album to smooth over the rivalries that had led to violent conflict in the rap world. He collaborated with West Coast rapper Too $hort on the song "Real N****z," which paid respects to both Tupac Shakur and The Notorious B.I.G. The lyrics declared that the East-West feud had gone too far when it resulted in the tragic deaths of such talented artists. Elsewhere on the album, JAY-Z asserted his claim to The Notorious B.I.G.'s throne in the track "The City Is Mine" featuring Blackstreet. Glenn Frey's "You Belong to the City" is sampled on the song, which has JAY-Z declaring he has paid his dues and is ready to take control.

Hip-hop fans cast their votes by snapping up more than 1 million copies of *Volume 1*, lifting it to the number 3 position on the Billboard 200 chart. Despite its popularity, however, JAY-Z later admitted that he was not altogether satisfied with the album. Of all his works, he said *Volume 1* was the one he wished he could do over again. "It was so close to being a classic, and I just put like three or four songs on there and messed it up,"[23] he noted.

"Hard Knock Life"

JAY-Z felt no such regrets about his next album, *Vol. 2 ... Hard Knock Life*. It sold more than 4 million copies, won a Grammy Award for Best Rap Album in 1999, and launched him to a new level of stardom. Anticipation for the album started building in the spring of 1998, when the first single was released. In "Hard Knock Life (Ghetto Anthem)," JAY-Z used samples from the children's chorus of the hit Broadway musical *Annie*. At first, in attempt to secure the rights for "Hard Knock Life," JAY-Z embellished the truth a bit when writing a letter to the original songwriters Charles Strouse and Martin Charnin. In hopes of convincing them to let him use the song, he told them when he was younger he had won an essay contest and gotten the chance to see the musical on Broadway; however, this was untrue. He had actually seen the TV version of *Annie* as a boy, and he remembered feeling inspired by the strength and courage of the characters—a group of poor children living in an orphanage. "These kids sing about the hard knock life, things everyone in the ghetto feels coming up," he explained. "That's the ghetto anthem."[24] After the songwriters granted him permission to use the song, JAY-Z decided to rap over the original version, adding lyrics about his own tough childhood.

"Hard Knock Life (Ghetto Anthem)" turned out to be a huge hit for JAY-Z. It dominated radio station playlists all summer long and created a surge of interest in the upcoming album. When *Vol. 2* was finally released on September 29, 1998, it debuted at number 1 on the Billboard album charts and remained in the top spot for five weeks. It produced a number of other hit singles as well, including "Can I Get a ...," "N**** What, N**** Who

(Originator 99)," and "Money Ain't a Thing."

JAY-Z collaborated with a number of well-known artists on *Vol. 2*. He used beats from hot producers such as Timbaland, Kid Capri, and Irv Gotti, and he featured vocals from guest rappers such as Foxy Brown, Jermaine Dupri, DMX, Ja Rule, and Memphis Bleek. In fact, JAY-Z only rapped by himself on two of the album's fourteen tracks. Some critics charged that he relied too heavily on the contributions of other artists, which diluted the overall impact of the album. "At his best, he shows no fear," wrote a reviewer for AllMusic. "Witness how the title track shamelessly works a Broadway showstopper from *Annie* into a raging ghetto cry, yet keeps it smooth enough for radio. It's a stunning single, but unfortunately, it promises more than the rest of the album can deliver."[25] Despite such criticism, however, *Vol. 2* turned JAY-Z into a dominant force in the world of hip-hop. *Rolling Stone* magazine recognized his position by naming him the Best Hip-Hop Artist of the Year for 1998.

JAY-Z launched a major concert tour in support of his third album. The *Hard Knock Life Tour*, also featuring DMX, Method Man, and Redman, sold out stadium-sized venues in all 52 cities it visited. Some cities were reluctant to host hip-hop concerts because they worried that the recent violence in the rap world would spill over to these events. However, JAY-Z's tour remained peaceful throughout its run, which helped open more concert venues to hardcore rap performers. In 2000, Roc-A-Fella released a documentary film about the *Hard Knock Life Tour* called *Backstage*, which was directed by Chris Fiore. In addition to concert footage, it gave viewers a behind-the-scenes look at JAY-Z and the other performers in the recording studio and on the road.

Conservative Criticisms

As JAY-Z rocketed to the top of the charts, he also became a target of criticism from conservative groups. These critics expressed concerns about some of the themes in JAY-Z's work and in rap music in general. They worried that young people who listened to *Vol. 2 … Hard Knock Life* might be influenced by JAY-Z's views about drugs and violence. The Christian group Focus on the

Hip-Hop History

Hip-hop music began with DJs at nightclubs and house parties. They played different records on two or more turntables at the same time and mixed the sounds together to create a new form of music. Before long, MCs added words to the beat. The vocal element of hip-hop music became known as rap.

The first rap recording hit the Top 40 on the Billboard charts in 1979. It was "Rapper's Delight" by the New Jersey-based Sugarhill Gang. By the mid-1980s, hip-hop music could be heard on radio stations across the country. The music industry recognized hip-hop's legitimacy in 1989, when *Billboard* magazine established a new category for rap records and the Recording Industry Association of America (RIAA) presented the first-ever Grammy Award for Best Rap Performance to DJ Jazzy Jeff and the Fresh Prince (Will Smith) for their

Family referred to the album as "garbage"[26] and warned parents not to let their children listen to it.

JAY-Z defended his work against such criticism. He argued that rappers had every right to write songs about drugs and violence because these things were common in their life experience. "We came up from the projects, urban neighborhoods," he explained. "It's not a coincidence that 80 percent of rappers have—if they didn't do it themselves—they've definitely seen somebody deal [drugs]. They was around it. They was in the car when it happened, they was in the hall when it happened. And then people condemn us for the music we make. All we doing is turning a light on in a dark place."[27]

JAY-Z claimed that he and other rap artists gave hip-hop fans greater insight into—and respect for—the problems facing poor African Americans living in the nation's largest cities. "I think song "Parents Just Don't Understand."

Although some critics insisted that rap music was a fad that would soon pass, its popularity grew throughout the 1990s and 2000s. Hip-hop culture gradually evolved to influence American fashion, language, and lifestyle. The best-known hip-hop artists became idols with the power to shape the thinking of a generation of young fans.

DJ Jazzy Jeff and the Fresh Prince's "Parents Just Don't Understand" was one of the first tracks that solidified hip-hop as a popular music genre.

the music speaks more directly to youth culture than any other music," he declared. "People that never lived [in the ghetto], they can just pick up a CD and experience the whole thing without having to get shot at."[28]

JAY-Z also dismissed the idea that listening to rap music would encourage fans to go out and deal drugs or commit violent crimes. "It's entertainment, and I trust the listener is smart enough to know that," he stated. "I'm just a human being. I do wrong things too and I hope you don't follow me."[29]

Criticism and Mixed Reviews

Amid this controversy in 1999, JAY-Z released the first single from his fourth album, *Vol. 3 … Life and Times of S. Carter.* The song, "Big Pimpin'," was a pop-oriented dance tune that featured several guest rappers. It became yet another in JAY-Z's string of hit records, but it also added fuel to fires of criticism surrounding the themes in his music. The lyrics to the song praised the lifestyle of pimps and made it sound acceptable to treat women disrespectfully.

When JAY-Z released *Vol. 3* on December 28, 1999, it received mixed reviews. Some critics felt that it was too slow and claimed that the lyrics were not as clever as those on *Vol. 2*. However, many others found the album to be a solid addition to JAY-Z's body of work. "This is his strongest album to date," wrote a reviewer for *Rolling Stone*, "with music that's filled with catchy hooks, rump-shaking beats and lyrics fueled by Jay's hustler's vigilance."[30] JAY-Z's growing fan base agreed with this assessment. They bought enough copies to lift *Vol. 3* to the top of the Billboard charts.

With four successful albums to his name, JAY-Z earned a spot among the most popular and influential stars in rap music. Some people wondered whether being rich and famous would hurt his credibility with hip-hop fans. JAY-Z acknowledged that his life had changed, but he insisted that he remained the same person he had been when he lived in the Marcy Houses. "With 5 million records out there, there are all kinds of things that you have to deal with," he noted. "People think that things change with you and start treating you differently. Street people start thinking that maybe you've gone soft. But I'm the same dude."[31]

Rocawear Clothing Line Launch

As JAY-Z's fame and popularity grew, he and his business partners took advantage of the opportunity to expand Roc-A-Fella Records into new areas. All three partners wanted Roc-A-Fella to be more than just a record label. They hoped to grow the business beyond music to tap into the surging popularity of hip-hop culture.

Many fans of rap music wanted to copy the image and lifestyle presented by their favorite stars, and they were willing to pay good money to do so. When the group Run-DMC appeared in music videos wearing Adidas sneakers, for example, many people rushed out to buy them. While Adidas benefited from the group's popularity, Run-DMC did not earn any money from the sales of the shoes. JAY-Z and his partners decided to develop their own clothing line so that they could keep the profits from this kind of cross-marketing opportunity.

In 1999, the Roc-A-Fella partners launched a line of urban fashions called Rocawear. Since they did not have any experience producing clothing, they initially considered making a deal with an established apparel manufacturer. In the end, though, they decided that they wanted more control—and more of the profits—than these companies were willing to offer. "In the beginning, we really wanted a deal with a clothing line because I would wear Iceberg [apparel] to shows and when we would get to shows, we'd see the entire audience in Iceberg. We went to Iceberg and wanted to make a deal with them, but at that point, we hadn't sold a significant amount of records," JAY-Z recalled. "When they didn't want to do the deal, we said, 'OK, we'll do it ourselves.'"[32]

JAY-Z and other well-known Roc-A-Fella artists wore Rocawear clothing in their concert appearances, interviews, photo sessions, and music videos. The artists increased the visibility and appeal of the Rocawear brand. Before long, hip-hop fans across the country were rushing out to buy the items they saw their favorite rappers wearing. Sales of Rocawear clothing took off, growing from $8 million in 1999 to $700 million in 2007. In March 2007, JAY-Z and his partners sold the rights of the clothing line to Iconix Brand Group for $204 million.

JAY-Z and his partners used a similar approach to expand Roc-A-Fella's business interests to include films. Many of the record

JAY-Z and his Roc-A-Fella partners started the clothing line Rocawear in 1999.

label's artists appeared in the 1998 movie, produced by Roc-A-Fella, *Streets Is Watching*, which was shot at the Marcy Houses in Brooklyn. Loosely based on JAY-Z's experiences, the film provided viewers with a gritty, realistic picture of life on the streets. The film incorporated a series of JAY-Z's unreleased music videos, along with performances from him and other rappers. Using JAY-Z's popularity to draw audiences to the film, *Streets Is Watching* brought increased exposure to other Roc-A-Fella artists and their music.

Stabbing at Kit Kat Club

By the end of 1999, JAY-Z's successful albums, concert tours, and business ventures had pushed him to the forefront of hip-hop culture. However, in December of that year, he was involved in a violent altercation that threatened everything he had worked hard to achieve. The incident occurred at a nightclub called the Kit Kat Club in Times Square in New York City. JAY-Z went there to help fellow rapper Q-Tip, a member of the group A Tribe Called Quest, celebrate the release of his solo album *Amplified*.

Many of the biggest names in rap music attended the star-studded event. One of the guests at the party was Lance "Un" Rivera of Untertainment Records. Several months earlier, Rivera had produced a song for JAY-Z, who was convinced that Rivera had sold bootleg copies of the record before it became available in stores. Although Rivera denied the charge, hard feelings still existed between the two men.

At one point in the evening, a fight broke out in the club. During the scuffle, Rivera was stabbed in the stomach and hit over the head with a champagne bottle. He claimed that JAY-Z was responsible for the attack. JAY-Z was arrested and charged with assault. Rivera also filed a civil lawsuit that, if successful, would force JAY-Z to pay monetary damages for Rivera's injuries and suffering.

The charges leveled at JAY-Z were very serious. If he was convicted, he faced up to 15 years in prison. However, JAY-Z consistently denied attacking Rivera. He said that he could produce eyewitnesses and a security video that proved he was nowhere near his rival when the fight broke out. The legal wrangling between the two sides dragged on for months, with every new development splashed across the pages of tabloid magazines.

Epiphany

As the legal drama surrounding the stabbing incident unfolded, Rivera became less confident about the identity of his attacker. He eventually dropped his civil lawsuit against JAY-Z, but the authorities still seemed determined to take the criminal case to trial. JAY-Z was convinced that the officials in charge of prosecuting the case enjoyed the attention that it brought them. "The DA [district attorney] has a publicist. Did you know that? That's unreal to me," he said. "That's not justice, that's drama."[33]

By the end of 2001, JAY-Z decided that he was tired of fighting and wanted the case to be over. He also expressed doubt that he would receive a fair trial because of his race, and he was not willing to take the risk of being convicted and sent to prison. "Where I grew up, I saw a lot of people get wronged," he claimed. "No matter how much you believe in the truth, that's always in the back of your mind."[34] Given all these considerations, JAY-Z agreed to plead guilty to a lesser charge and accepted a punishment of three years' probation.

JAY-Z later claimed that the whole experience affected his outlook on life. He realized that he could have lost everything he had worked so hard to achieve. It made him appreciate his success in a deeper way, and it made him determined to be more careful in the future. "That was the turning point for me," he acknowledged. "It was like, 'O.K., this can all go away fast. You work hard for years, and it can all go away in a night. Slow down, big boy. Think.'"[35]

himself on *The Blueprint* as the god of the rap world. He introduced himself as "J-Hova" or "H.O.V.A.," taken from Jehovah—the proper name of God from the Old Testament of the Bible. In a review for *Rolling Stone*, Neil Strauss claimed that JAY-Z may have felt compelled to build himself up after all the negative publicity that surrounded the assault case. "There's something about being persecuted, or at least believing oneself to be persecuted, that makes people embrace and reaffirm their own identity—witness JAY-Z's sixth album, *The Blueprint*," he wrote. "Personal and legal problems have provoked JAY-Z to write what may be his most personal, straightforward album but also his most self-aggrandizing work."[37]

Rapper Feuds

Besides his legal troubles, JAY-Z had other reasons to feel a need to defend himself on *The Blueprint*. His many successes had drawn the attention of rival rappers, and he had become a major target for insults and threats in the ongoing battle of words in the rap world. Although the bitter feud between East Coast and West Coast rappers had ended following the violent deaths of Tupac Shakur and The Notorious B.I.G., new rivalries developed between various artists vying for supremacy on the East Coast scene. A number of fellow New York rappers attacked JAY-Z in their work, including Jadakiss, DMX, Nas, and the late Prodigy of Mobb Deep.

The heated exchanges between JAY-Z and Nas turned their two-year-long battle into one of the most famous rap feuds in history. The two rappers traded jabs in interviews, at concert appearances, and on the radio. JAY-Z made his feelings about Nas clear in "Takeover," the opening track on *The Blueprint*. The song had a military beat and featured a sample from the Doors song "Five to One." The lyrics questioned Nas's street credibility and suggested that he had invented his ghetto background. JAY-Z also attacked Nas's talent as a rapper and claimed that his latest releases belonged in the trash. Finally, JAY-Z asserted his own superiority and presented himself as the dominant figure on the New York rap scene.

JAY-Z insisted that his attacks on Nas and other rivals were simply part of the battle-rap tradition. He claimed that he ignored their insults as long as possible but finally had to fight back in order to gain their respect. "Everybody wants to be respected," he explained. "Even if we're not friends, we gotta respect each other. And I felt I was bein' disrespected by them, so I had to show them. And I really waited it out because I didn't want people to think I was a bully. Because I have the ear of a lot more people than them. You have to be very careful with that power … I'm sure they respect me right now."[38]

Shortly after the release of *The Blueprint*, Nas answered "Takeover" in his song "Ether." He focused his criticism on the sexist lyrics and attitudes he saw in JAY-Z's work. He insinuated that these themes showed that JAY-Z felt some deep-seated anger or fear toward women. JAY-Z responded to "Ether" with "Super Ugly," a freestyle rap that first aired on a New York radio station. In this song, JAY-Z viciously attacked Nas by claiming that he had an affair with Carmen Bryan, the mother of Nas's child.

Although the two rappers continued to exchange slight verbal blows afterward, "Super Ugly" marked the end of their all-out feud. Many people felt that JAY-Z had gone overboard in the song. Even his own mother called to tell him that she found it mean-spirited and that he should apologize. Nas never responded to the song formally, although he did make critical comments about it in interviews. The conflict eventually faded to the point that the two rappers decided to make peace. Both JAY-Z and Nas agreed to perform at a 2005 concert sponsored by a New York radio station. The two rappers made a joint appearance on stage and shook hands to officially bring their feud to a close.

The Blueprint 2

JAY-Z continued to discuss some of the negative aspects of fame in his next album, *The Blueprint 2: The Gift and the Curse*. By November 12, 2002, when the album was released, he had settled the assault case and cooled his battle of words with Nas.

However, JAY-Z still faced the challenge of maintaining his identity—which had been forged by poverty and pain—while

also enjoying the rewards of his success. This struggle became the overall theme of *The Blueprint 2*. "The gift-versus-curse concept helps hold things together," noted Christian Hoard, a reviewer for *Rolling Stone*, "as Jay wows you with his jet-setting lifestyle one minute, then contemplates the darker side of fame and his ghetto upbringing the next."[39]

The first collaboration between JAY-Z and Beyoncé was "'03 Bonnie & Clyde," which was included on the rapper's album *The Blueprint 2: The Gift and the Curse*.

By all appearances, JAY-Z had a great deal to say on the subject. *The Blueprint 2* was a double album, containing 25 tracks and employing the talents of many producers and guest vocalists. It spawned several hit singles, including "'03 Bonnie & Clyde" (a duet with Beyoncé) and "Guns and Roses" (a duet with Lenny Kravitz), and sold an impressive 4 million copies.

Despite its strong sales, *The Blueprint 2* was not nearly as popular with critics as its predecessor. Many reviewers complained that the double album was too long and unfocused. They claimed that it only contained enough quality material for a single album. JAY-Z responded to this criticism five months later by releasing the compilation album *The Blueprint 2.1*. This album contained half of the tracks from *The Blueprint 2*, along with two previously unreleased songs.

Retiring from Rap

With the release of *The Blueprint 2.1* in 2003, JAY-Z's albums had collectively sold more than 30 million copies. Although he seemed to have a magic touch for connecting with hip-hop fans, he recognized that this might not be the case as he grew older. "I think, unfortunately, rap music is made to destroy itself," he stated. "You have to be fresh and sell to an audience that's 16 to 25. They demand that you 'keep it hood,' 'keep it real.'"[40]

JAY-Z's success as a recording artist, meanwhile, had provided him with numerous opportunities to expand his business interests. His Rocawear clothing brand had posted an incredible $300 million in sales in 2003 alone. The company planned to expand its inventory to include new lines of apparel for women and children. In addition, JAY-Z became one of the main backers of a chain of sports bars called the 40/40 Club that opened in New York City in 2003 and Atlantic City, New Jersey, in 2005. This was followed by locations opening in Las Vegas in 2007; at the Barclays Center in Brooklyn in 2012; and at Hartsfield–Jackson Atlanta International Airport in Atlanta, Georgia, in 2014. The Atlantic City location closed in 2013, and the Las Vegas location closed in 2008.

JAY-Z also found himself in demand among companies that wanted him to endorse their products. He accepted an offer from Reebok to help design and promote his own signature line of shoes, the S. Carter collection. JAY-Z thus became the first celebrity from outside the world of sports to have his own athletic shoe. The first model introduced by Reebok in 2003 sold out within a week, making it the fastest-selling shoe in the company's history at that time.

Between managing his business empire and promoting new artists on the Roc-A-Fella record label, JAY-Z found that he did not have much time to devote to making new albums.

JAY-Z is shown here with rapper Memphis Bleek, who at one time was considered to be JAY-Z's protégé, at the opening of the 40/40 Club in New York City.

He eventually decided to retire as a recording artist to concentrate on new challenges. "I've had it with the rap game. Time to focus on other things. That's why I'm retiring," he explained. "I've talked about wanting to have enough to get out since my first album. I was always more interested in the business side."[41]

The "Final Album"

Determined to go out on top, JAY-Z began working on his farewell album, which he called *The Black Album*. He decided to return to his roots and create a prequel to his first album, *Reasonable Doubt*. *The Black Album* was released on November 14, 2003. The opening track, called "December 4th," after his birthday, featured spoken-word interludes from his mother. Later tracks continued to tell the story of his life.

Critics described *The Black Album* as an honest and

introspective work that stood as a fitting conclusion for JAY-Z's recording career. "Given one last chance to make an impact, JAY-Z has come up with one of the better albums of his career,"[42] noted a reviewer for *Rolling Stone*. *The Black Album* sold 3 million copies and spawned a number of hit singles, including "What More Can I Say," "Change Clothes," and "99 Problems," which earned JAY-Z a Grammy Award for Best Rap Solo Performance.

The Black Album also featured the dance tune "Dirt Off Your Shoulder," which entered mainstream popular culture in a way that few rap songs ever had before. JAY-Z's lyrics suggested that the best way for people to deal with criticism was to brush it off, like they would brush a speck of dirt from their shoulder. This idea became the basis for a brushing gesture that could be used in response to critics. In 2008, then-Senator Barack Obama even used the gesture during his successful presidential campaign to show how he intended to deal with criticism from his political rivals.

A Memorable Farewell Concert

JAY-Z followed up on the success of *The Black Album* by announcing that he would end his career with a triumphant farewell concert, with all the proceeds donated to charity. The *Fade to Black* concert was scheduled for November 25, 2003, at Madison Square Garden in New York City. This premier concert venue had not hosted a show by a hip-hop artist in 15 years due to concerns about the potential for violence. However, when JAY-Z convinced the Garden to make an exception for his final concert, the 20,000 seats sold out in less than 5 minutes.

The *Fade to Black* concert was a star-studded event, from the famous faces in the audience to the wealth of talented performers on

Fade to Black was a documentary about JAY-Z's final concert at Madison Square Garden before his retirement in 2003.

Performing with
Paul McCartney

Mixing different kinds of music together is an important element of hip-hop. In recognition of this, JAY-Z and other rap artists often make stripped-down versions of their songs available for other artists to sample in their work. For example, JAY-Z released the vocal tracks from *The Black Album*—without the accompanying music—in hopes that other rappers would use them in mash-ups and mixes.

A British DJ known as Danger Mouse combined the raps from JAY-Z's *The Black Album* with samples from the classic Beatles release titled *The Beatles*, but known as "The White Album" because of the white cover. The result became known as *The Grey Album*, which was released in February 2004. As it turned out, though, Danger Mouse did not have permission from EMI—the label that held the legal rights to the Beatles music—to use songs from "The White Album." EMI filed a legal action to force the DJ and record sellers to stop

stage. The show featured guest appearances by many of JAY-Z's friends and collaborators, including Mary J. Blige, Beyoncé, Missy Elliott, Foxy Brown, R. Kelly, Ghostface Killah, Pharrell Williams, and Beanie Sigel. JAY-Z even invited the mothers of the late rappers Tupac Shakur and The Notorious B.I.G., Afeni Shakur and Voletta Wallace, to join him on stage. He delighted the crowd by playing songs from his entire career, changing his costume five times, and using lots of pyrotechnics.

The spectacular show formed the basis of the 2004 documentary film *Fade to Black*, which also featured behind-the-scenes footage of the performers. JAY-Z claimed that he did not fully appreciate the impact of the event until he watched the movie.

distributing *The Grey Album*. The swirl of controversy surrounding the album only increased its popularity, however, and it became a huge underground hit.

Inspired by *The Grey Album*, other enterprising music lovers created *The Grey Video*. This popular internet movie combined footage from various JAY-Z

JAY-Z, Paul McCartney, and Linkin Park performed together at the 48th Grammy Awards.

music videos with footage from the Beatles' film *A Hard Day's Night*. At least one former Beatle seemed to appreciate the connection with JAY-Z. Paul McCartney agreed to appear on stage with the rap star at the 48th Grammy Awards. They performed an innovative combination of the Beatles song "Yesterday" with the song "Numb/Encore" by JAY-Z and Linkin Park.

"I couldn't feel it at the time. It took for me to watch the movie to really say like 'Wow, that was huge,'" he said. "The emotional aspect kicked in later when I looked at it … I was blown away."[43] He felt that the film did a great job of tracing the journey "of a kid from Marcy Projects in Brooklyn making it to the biggest stage in the world."[44]

Chapter **Four**

Building a Business Empire

When JAY-Z announced his retirement in 2003, some fans worried that he was leaving the music business entirely. They thought that his popularity and influence would fade if he stopped rapping and expressed hope that he would reconsider. As it turned out, their fears about JAY-Z's retirement were unfounded. JAY-Z continued to record and perform with other artists. In addition, he made a dramatic move to become one of the most powerful figures in the recording industry. He proved he was capable of navigating many other facets of the music business and would eventually transform himself into a music mogul.

In 2004, he accepted a position as president of Def Jam Records. During his three-year tenure in this position, JAY-Z gained even more credibility and respect, helped open new doors for black executives, and proved to the masses he

JAY-Z became close friends with Rick Rubin (left) and Russell Simmons (right) when he became the new president of Def Jam Records.

was more than just a rapper and could achieve success in several sectors within the music industry.

Retirement Life

Even after he officially retired as a recording artist, JAY-Z stayed busy. A 2004 *New York Times* profile described him as "the hardest-working retiree in the music industry."[45] Although JAY-Z did not release any new albums under his own name, he continued recording songs with other artists. In 2003, he collaborated with Beyoncé on the hit song "Crazy in Love." It won two Grammy Awards—Best R&B Song and Best Rap/Sung Collaboration— in 2004. Their performance also fueled intense speculation in the media about whether the two stars were romantically involved. That same year, JAY-Z received further recognition of his talents as an artist when he earned the Golden Note Award from the American Society of Composers, Authors, and Publishers (ASCAP).

JAY-Z also collaborated with R&B star R. Kelly on the album *Unfinished Business* during his retirement. It debuted at the number 1 position on the Billboard charts upon its release in 2004. The two artists also planned a 40-city concert tour in support of the album. "Unfortunately, what looked good on paper didn't work out that way in reality,"[46] according to JAY-Z. As soon as they hit the road, the two stars clashed repeatedly. After a few concerts together, JAY-Z kicked R. Kelly off the tour for unprofessional behavior. "It takes a lot to make Jay mad," a friend noted, "so the fact that this got to the boiling point shows how bad it was."[47] JAY-Z filled the remaining concert dates with a string of other featured music artists, including Usher and Mary J. Blige. R. Kelly later filed a $75 million lawsuit, arguing that JAY-Z had broken a contract by forcing him to leave the tour. A judge decided that there was not enough evidence to make a ruling and threw out the case.

In 2006, he won another Grammy Award for Best Rap/Sung

Collaboration for "Numb/Encore." This song combined parts of the JAY-Z song "Encore" with parts of the song "Numb" by the hard-rock band Linkin Park. It was one of several mash-ups of existing songs by the artists that appeared on the collaboration album *Collision Course*, which was released in November 2004. *Collision Course* was a huge hit with fans. It debuted at number 1 on the Billboard charts and included a DVD with footage of JAY-Z and Linkin Park performing some of the songs live on MTV. JAY-Z was still performing "Numb/Encore" years later; in 2017, however, it was for a tragic reason. That year, the music world experienced another tragedy with the suicide of Linkin Park singer Chester Bennington. After his death, JAY-Z performed "Numb/Encore" at several festival appearances, such as V Festival and Made In America Festival, and dedicated each performance to Bennington. JAY-Z also took that opportunity to speak about the importance of addressing mental health issues.

New Challenges

Although JAY-Z enjoyed his post-retirement musical collaborations, he still looked for opportunities to challenge himself in other ways. He was particularly interested in expanding his role as a business executive in the recording industry. "The business … has always been something I focused on, and rightly so," he explained. "Rap is a young man's game, and I thought about that even when I was young—it has to come to an end. Whatever job you have, be it hustling on the street or working at the mall, you gotta have a plan for when it's over."[48]

JAY-Z had gained valuable experience in the music business by running the Roc-A-Fella label. He hoped that this background—combined with the credibility and influence he had built within the industry as a successful rapper—might help him land a powerful position with one of America's giant record companies. Many people in the music business supported the idea. "Who wouldn't want to hire the most popular guy in hip-hop? His face alone would get the deal done," noted one industry executive. "That wouldn't have happened to a kid coming straight out of the ghetto—he never would have had a shot."[49]

New President of Def Jam

By the time JAY-Z became president of the company in January 2005, Def Jam Records had been at the forefront of hip-hop music and culture for two decades. Russell Simmons and Rick Rubin had founded the record label in 1984 in a dormitory room at New York University. Def Jam earned its trend-setting reputation by promoting such early hip-hop stars as Run-DMC, LL Cool J, the Beastie Boys, and Public Enemy. The company signed a distribution deal with Columbia Records in 1985 and grew rapidly in both size and influence.

JAY-Z's first interaction with Def Jam came in 1997. Shortly after the release of his first album, he and his partners at Roc-A-Fella Records signed a joint venture agreement with the larger label. As part of their deal, the two companies also agreed to share ownership rights to all original or master recordings. As JAY-Z released more albums and became a major star, Def Jam benefited from his success.

In 1999, Universal Music Group bought Def Jam. Thanks to strong record sales by JAY-Z and other artists on the label, such as Ludacris, Ja Rule, and Kanye West, Def Jam posted $1 billion in revenue in 2004. That year, however, a number of top executives left Universal and moved to rival Warner Music Group. Concerned that JAY-Z and other Roc-A-Fella artists might be tempted to change labels, Universal cemented the relationship by making JAY-Z the new president of Def Jam.

Still, JAY-Z was not willing to accept a position that used only his image, rather than his talents. He wanted a hands-on management position that would allow him to influence the future direction of hip-hop music and make a difference in the black community. "What I want to do is have a position that opens the doors for black executives in the music business," he stated. "I don't think there are enough of us. I want to break that glass ceiling. But it has to be a real position, or I'm not doing it. I want to be the black quarterback."[50]

Record Label Shake-Up

Around the time that JAY-Z retired as an artist, a management shake-up occurred at Universal Music Group (UMG). UMG was a giant company in the music industry, with dozens of respected record labels, a huge roster of top artists from all genres of music, and an extensive catalog of copyrighted songs under its control. UMG also was the parent company of Def Jam Records, which owned half of Roc-A-Fella Records through a 1997 joint venture agreement.

In 2004, several top executives left UMG and moved to rival Warner Music Group. Some of these executives had been involved with Def Jam since the label's early years, and they maintained close relationships with many Def Jam and Roc-A-Fella artists. This event led to industry rumors that JAY-Z and other rappers would move to Warner, following the executives who had long supported them.

Antonio "L. A." Reid, who became chairman of UMG's Island Def Jam Music Group after the management shake-up, was determined to prevent this from happening. He recognized that the key to keeping existing Def Jam and Roc-A-Fella artists in the fold was to include JAY-Z more prominently within the business side of the company. "Jay being the biggest, most successful, most influential artist on the roster, it became a priority of mine to develop

L. A. Reid (center) realized JAY-Z was an asset to Def Jam Records as both an artist and a businessman.

a relationship,"[51] Reid explained.

When Reid learned that JAY-Z was looking for an executive position, he offered the rapper a prestigious job as president of Def Jam Records. "After 10 years of successfully running Roc-A-Fella, Shawn has proved himself to be an astute businessman, in addition to the brilliant artistic talent that the world sees and hears," Reid said in an official press release announcing JAY-Z's appointment. "I can think of no one more relevant and credible in the hip-hop community to build upon Def Jam's fantastic legacy and move the company into its next groundbreaking era."[52]

To convince JAY-Z to take the job, UMG made him a huge offer. As part of the deal, Def Jam purchased the half of Roc-A-Fella that it did not already own for $10 million. The company also offered to pay JAY-Z a salary estimated between $6 million and $8 million per year. Most importantly, UMG agreed to give JAY-Z full control of his master recordings—along with all the future profits that came from these copyrighted songs—after 10 years. Between the financial arrangements and the opportunity to become the first popular artist to take the reins of a major record label, JAY-Z could not resist. He signed a three-year contract to serve as president of Def Jam, beginning in January 2005.

Reid insisted that his company got a good deal as well. "Def Jam is the number one hip-hop label in the world," he stated. "Having Jay says that the legacy continues. If you're a 16-year-old rapper in Brooklyn or Atlanta or Houston, and you know that Jay-Z carries on the legacy of hip-hop, then Def Jam becomes your preferred destination."[53]

Job Insecurities

Upon moving into his luxurious executive office in the Universal Building, JAY-Z realized that he faced high expectations in his new job. "It's the biggest hip-hop label of all time," he said of Def Jam. "If that thing falls apart, it's on my head. I was naive enough to believe I can do it."[54] JAY-Z also understood that many people questioned whether he had the necessary skills and qualifications to succeed in such a high-profile position. "Any record executive knows that Jay-Z in the boardroom brings another level of respect from within the industry," said the vice president of another record label. "But the real key isn't just whether or not Jay-Z is able to find and sign the talent. It's whether he can really do the business part, which means staying within budget and bringing in a certain amount of revenue. That's the test for Jay."[55]

JAY-Z was able to draw upon his experience running Roc-A-Fella in adjusting to the demands of his new job. He also received a great deal of help and support from within Def Jam and UMG. UMG management handled most of the high-level contracts, budgets, and financial arrangements for him. JAY-Z also had a staff of seven division heads within Def Jam to take care of the day-to-day aspects of running the business. This left JAY-Z free to focus on what he knew best: the music side of the business. His main job involved finding new artists and turning them into stars. "His opinion of music and his point of view on marketing is absolutely spot on," said Steve Stoute, former head of the urban music division of Interscope Records at UMG. "I don't know who wouldn't want to work for him."[56]

Within months of settling into his new job, JAY-Z signed a number of talented newcomers to record deals with Def Jam, including Young Jeezy, Ne-Yo, Rihanna, and British rapper Lady Sovereign. He also promoted new albums, videos, and concert tours that turned existing artists such as Kanye West and Ludacris into huge stars. JAY-Z developed close relationships with many of these artists, and he found it very rewarding to nurture their careers. "I'm not looking to be anybody's boss. I'm just looking to help the process. If they win, I win,"[57] he explained. "I love the process. It's another way of being creative. Especially with a new artist, when somebody walks in and they don't understand what's going on and they are all wide-eyed. Then the next year, they are signing autographs and they're big, too."[58]

Innovation in Hip-Hop

On a typical day at the office, JAY-Z spent several hours scanning radio playlists and album charts, listening to new songs, and advising his artists about career moves. "If Jay-Z says you have to go back in the studio and write new bars, you've got to write new bars," said Semtex, the former urban promotions manager for Def Jam. "If Jay-Z says your stage show isn't hot, it isn't hot. You can't argue with him; he's sold millions of records."[59]

Over time, JAY-Z used his position as head of Def Jam to shift hip-hop culture toward a more mature, sophisticated style. His fans took note of the fact that one of the most successful rappers of all time quit performing to become a recording executive. This decision made the world of business seem cooler and more interesting to many of them. Some of this change in attitude became clear in the subject matter addressed in rap lyrics and the clothing worn by hip-hop fans. "In 'getting his executive on,' as the kids call it these days," wrote one analyst, JAY-Z "is not only redirecting the hip-hop culture he helped popularize—from hooded sweatshirt thug-chic to button-down-shirt sophistication—but injecting the music business with a new sensibility."[60]

With JAY-Z as president, Def Jam solidified its position as the most popular and influential hip-hop label. "It's been great," he stated in late 2006. "The first year we had the No. 2 market share and this year, if everything goes right, we'll have the No. 1."[61] The management of Def Jam's parent company, UMG, expressed great satisfaction with JAY-Z's performance. "Jay's put Def Jam back on the map," said former UMG executive Doug Morris. "Everything he touches gets cooler."[62]

Chapter Five

The Comeback

Even though being the head of Def Jam was rewarding, JAY-Z felt compelled to end his retirement and return to the recording studio. He had delved into the business side of the music industry and was yearning to tap back into his creative side. Originally, he thought he was too old to remain a staple in the rap world but later realized he had more to offer the genre, and he solidified his staying power.

His long-awaited comeback album, *Kingdom Come*, was followed by an ambitious, Grammy-nominated concept album inspired by the movie *American Gangster*. By combining business successes with artistic accomplishments, JAY-Z brought the various threads of his career together to reach a new level of power and influence. He also expressed a growing recognition that he could use his wealth and celebrity to have a positive impact on the world.

Returning from Retirement

During his first year as president of Def Jam in 2005, JAY-Z mostly concentrated on his new role and responsibilities as an executive. He continued to come up with ideas for songs and albums that he might want to record someday, but he did not feel a strong desire to return to the studio.

JAY-Z did perform in concert on a few occasions during this period, though. A memorable example came in October 2005, when he headlined the annual Powerhouse concert for the New York radio station Power 105.1. A number of other top Def Jam artists appeared as well, including Kanye West, Young Jeezy, and Ne-Yo. Since the concert was called *I Declare War*, many people assumed that JAY-Z would use the show to launch verbal attacks at his biggest rivals. Instead, he made a strong statement that his new executive position placed him above the fray of rap battles.

During the show, JAY-Z presented himself as the president of the United States. He sat behind a large desk on a stage set that looked like the Oval Office in the White House. Surrounded by actors dressed as Secret Service agents in suits, he declared his intention to make peace in the rap world. The highlight of the show came when his longtime rival Nas joined him onstage to officially bring their years-long feud to an end. The two artists performed a mash-up of JAY-Z's song "Dead Presidents" and Nas's song "The World Is Yours."

The thrill that JAY-Z felt from these performances made him realize that he needed more than an occasional collaboration or concert appearance to satisfy his love for creating music.

In 2006, less than three years after he retired, JAY-Z returned to the recording studio. "It was the worst retirement, maybe, in history," he acknowledged. Upon returning, he claimed that it "wasn't like a defining moment … Something, when you love it, is always tugging at you and itching at you, and I was putting it off and putting it off … I started fumbling around to see if it felt good."[63]

As the president of Def Jam, JAY-Z had access to an all-star group of producers and collaborators, including Dr. Dre, Kanye West, the Neptunes, Chris Martin of Coldplay, John Legend, Usher, Ne-Yo, and Beyoncé. All of these artists were eager to help him with his long-awaited comeback album. JAY-Z named the album *Kingdom Come*, after an old DC Comics series in which Superman returned to Earth after a self-imposed exile to find destruction and chaos. Fans

Nas and JAY-Z ended their longtime feud during the Powerhouse concert at the Continental Airlines Arena in East Rutherford, New Jersey, in 2005.

snapped up copies upon its release on November 21, 2006. *Kingdom Come* debuted at number 1 on the Billboard album chart, selling 680,000 copies in the first week, and went on to top 2 million in sales.

The album spawned several hit singles, including "Show Me What You Got." Many of the songs on the album featured samples from an interesting variety of music. The title track included samples from Rick James's funky dance tune "Super Freak," for instance, while "Oh My God" had samples from Genya Raven's "Whipping Post." To the dismay of some fans who had enjoyed JAY-Z's take on street life, many of his lyrics focused on the rewards of being a high-powered executive. "It wasn't what people wanted to hear," JAY-Z acknowledged. "But it's what I wanted to do. I was trying to show that hip-hop can talk about different things."[64]

Kingdom Come received mixed reviews from critics. Most reviewers agreed that the album had some strong points, but they generally found that JAY-Z's long-awaited comeback failed to live up to expectations. "*Kingdom Come* was hardly the creative flop it was cracked up to be, but it never had a prayer of living up to everybody's hopes," noted one reviewer. "People don't just expect new records from Jay—they expect epochal events, game-changing statements. Yet Jay's retirement put his myth-building on pause."[65]

Film Inspiration

After the release of *Kingdom Come*, JAY-Z did not expect to make another album for a while. He was prepared to turn his full attention back to his job at Def Jam. In mid-2007, however, he was inspired to make a new album that returned him to his roots.

The inspiration came from an unusual source: a movie called *American Gangster*. The film was based on the story of Frank Lucas, a real-life gangster who built a heroin empire in Harlem, New York, during the 1970s. It starred Denzel Washington as Lucas and Russell Crowe as the New York City police detective who was determined to bring him to justice.

JAY-Z was invited to an advance screening of the film. He was struck by the parallels with his own story. "The way Denzel portrayed the character was very laid back, and I saw similar traits in my personality," he explained. "But mostly, I just pulled emotions from the film and not so much his particular story. It was the complexity of the human beings that I was drawn to. For most of the movie, you don't know who is the good guy or bad guy."[66]

Watching *American Gangster* inspired JAY-Z to envision how his life might have turned out if he had remained a drug dealer rather than becoming a rapper. Before long, he was actively sketching out a concept album, or an album that is based around a certain theme, that explored this fantasy. He approached Sean "Diddy" Combs to serve as the producer. As it turned out, Combs had been saving a number of good background beats in case a suitable project came along. "I was like, 'Wow, what are you doing with all this stuff?'" JAY-Z remembered. "And he was like, 'Who is going to rap on this but you?'"[67]

American Gangster *Release*

The resulting album also was called *American Gangster*, even though none of the songs appeared on the soundtrack of the film. It hit the top of the Billboard charts upon its release on November 6, 2007. This gave JAY-Z 10 career number-1 albums, which tied him with Elvis Presley for the most ever by a solo performer. (As of 2018, the Beatles hold the overall record with 19.)

The songs on *American Gangster* followed the rise and fall of an imagined drug lord. "Jay's *Gangster* tale follows a striking, dramatic arc of its own, transporting listeners from a young hustler's ambition ('Pray,' 'No Hook') to a kingpin's arrogance ('Roc Boys,' 'Ignorant S—') to a career criminal's inevitable ruin ('Fallin'),"[68] Simon Vozick-Levinson wrote in *Entertainment Weekly*. Since the album was intended to tell a story, JAY-Z did not make the songs available separately as singles. "It's a concept album, not a collection of singles, and I want it heard the way I intended it," he explained. "A painter doesn't sell a section of a painting. He sells a whole body of work."[69]

American Gangster received glowing reviews from critics, who praised the album's originality and passion. "Having a fictional character to play around with gets Jay out of his post-retirement rut," Rob Sheffield, a reviewer for *Rolling Stone*, wrote. "Frank Lucas fires his imagination … [and] helps push the artist outside his own head."[70] JAY-Z appreciated the fact that *American Gangster*—which earned a Grammy nomination for Best Rap Album—helped restore his reputation as a top recording artist:

> "With rap, it's always about the next project, no matter who you are! It's about what's current, what's happening right this second," he noted. "[Gangster] set the foundation all over again, and it made everybody say, Whoa, hold up for a second. It quelled those arguments [that Jay had fallen off], and those arguments were not founded, but that's just how it happens. That's what keeps it fresh for me. I love that challenge."[71]

In Search of New Business Opportunities

Shortly after the release of *American Gangster*, JAY-Z's love of new challenges led him to make another dramatic career move. When his three-year contract with Def Jam expired at the end of 2007, he stepped down as president of the label. He explained that this decision was prompted in part by his rekindled enthusiasm for making new music. However, he also wanted to pursue new business opportunities within the music industry that moved beyond the traditional framework of record labels. "The record business is in trouble, not the music business," he stated. "People are always gonna make music. But the record business, they've got some things to fix."[72]

In early 2008, JAY-Z made a deal with the concert promoter Live Nation worth an estimated $150 million. In addition to organizing, promoting, and selling tickets to live shows by JAY-Z, Live Nation also planned to distribute his albums, market his merchandise, and handle other aspects of his career. JAY-Z felt that Live Nation's consolidated approach gave it many different ways to reach consumers and keep up with rapid changes in the music industry. "Everyone's trying to figure it out," he said. "I want to be on the front lines in that fight."[73]

Most importantly for JAY-Z, the Live Nation deal included financing that allowed him to create his own entertainment venture, Roc Nation. One of JAY-Z's first priorities for Roc Nation was to form a new record label. In 2008, he joined forces with two Norwegian entrepreneurs—Tor Erik Hermansen and Mikkel Storleer Eriksen, who owned a music production company called Stargate—to create StarRoc. JAY-Z's role with the new label was similar to the role he played at Def Jam: finding and promoting new talent.

Outside of the music industry, JAY-Z took a leading role in bringing a National Basketball Association (NBA) franchise to Brooklyn. After he became part owner of the New Jersey Nets in 2003, he helped negotiate a deal to move the team to a new stadium called the Barclays Center in New York City in 2012. He believed that having an NBA team would bring jobs, money, hope, and pride to Brooklyn.

"For a kid growing up in the Marcy Projects to be involved with a professional basketball team is way beyond anyone's dream," he said. "You may think you can make it to the NBA, and that's a lofty dream. You never have the dream that you're gonna own the team."[74]

Philanthropy

As he branched out into new areas of business, JAY-Z decided to sell his successful Rocawear clothing line to Iconix for $204 million. The deal significantly increased the rap star's net worth. As of 2017, *Forbes* magazine states his net worth is an estimated $810 million. Recalling his humble beginnings, JAY-Z felt a responsibility to use some of his enormous wealth to help others. "We're the first generation of hip-hop guys to really make the big money," he acknowledged. "The generation before us never made this type of cash, so it's on us to keep it going and give it back."[75] Longing to have a positive impact on the world, JAY-Z actively supported a number of charitable causes. He spearheaded an annual toy drive, for instance, to ensure that kids in the Marcy Houses received gifts for Christmas. He also donated time and money to help people affected by the New York City terrorist attacks of September 11, 2001, and people left homeless by Hurricane Katrina in 2005. JAY-Z also became involved in efforts to address the global water crisis through MTV's Water for Life program. To help raise awareness of the cause, he appeared in a

Glastonbury Festival
Controversy

Even as the popularity of hip-hop exploded around the world, some corners of the music scene remained steadfastly anti-rap. JAY-Z received a clear reminder of this attitude in February 2008, when he agreed to headline the famous Glastonbury Festival in England. First organized in the 1970s, the annual performing arts event featured live music by rock, folk, and alternative artists, as well as dance, comedy, and theatrical performances.

JAY-Z was the most prominent hip-hop artist ever invited to Glastonbury, so naturally, his invitation created controversy as soon as the organizers announced it. Noel Gallagher, former lead singer of the alternative-rock band Oasis, criticized the festival organizers for including JAY-Z among the headliners. "I'm sorry, but Jay-Z? No chance. Glastonbury has a tradition of guitar music," he said. "I'm not having hip hop at Glastonbury. It's wrong."[1] Although some festival organizers and ticketholders agreed with Gallagher, many others spoke up on behalf of JAY-Z. His supporters argued that video for MTV, gave a series of interviews, and spoke at the United Nations (UN) in 2006. In all of these public appearances, JAY-Z cited statistics showing that 1.1 billion people around the world lacked access to safe drinking water. "As I started looking around and looking at ways that I could become helpful, it started at the first thing—water, something as simple as water," he said at a news conference. "It took very little, very little to see these numbers."[76]

In 2006 JAY-Z traveled to Africa, where he visited poor villages that suffered from severe water shortages. He felt honored to provide pumps that supplied the residents with clean water. "I've given money and written checks," he noted, "but when you're on

hip-hop was a legitimate musical genre that deserved to be showcased at Glastonbury. They noted that JAY-Z was an international superstar who could increase the festival's appeal for young audiences.

When the festival finally took place, JAY-Z made a dramatic musical response to the criticism. He appeared on stage accompanied by two acoustic guitar players and led the crowd in a rousing version of Oasis's biggest hit song, "Wonderwall." "Jay-Z took the Oasis star's criticism and turned it into one of the great Glastonbury moments," wrote one reviewer. "It was a moment that will surely go down in festival folklore."[2]

1. Quoted in Colin Paterson, "Hip-Hop 'Wrong' for Glastonbury," BBC News, April 14, 2008. news.bbc.co.uk/1/hi/entertainment/7345780.stm.

2. Quoted in "A Glastonbury Legend Is Born," The Independent, June 28, 2008. www.independent.co.uk/arts-entertainment/music/news/a-glastonbury-legend-is-born-856654.html.

JAY-Z performed at Glastonbury Festival in 2008, despite criticisms from other artists who did not want a hip-hop act to be included in the lineup.

Shawn Carter Foundation

In 2003, JAY-Z and his mother, Gloria, founded the Shawn Carter Foundation. After being retired for a year, Gloria was looking for something to keep her busy. In her previous job, she had trained young people and became a mentor for them. After being invited to one of her trainees' graduations and having him recognize her impact in his life, she decided she wanted to continue to mentor young individuals.

"We all need to do something because you can't sit around and expect everyone else to do something when you don't do anything," Gloria said. "So I called my son and said ... 'We need to give back to the community. We need to start a scholarship fund because there's so many kids out there that want to go to school but don't have the money to go because they're underserved.'"[1]

The charity is dedicated to helping individuals from low-income backgrounds further their educations at institutions of higher learning. As of 2018, the organization has raised more than $4 million to be used toward programs supporting initiatives to empower youth and

the ground and you turn on the faucet and the village get water for the first time, it's like nothing else."[77]

JAY-Z also felt a responsibility to be a positive role model for his young fans. He often visited schools and encouraged the students to believe in themselves and reach for their dreams. However, JAY-Z always told his young audiences that his own path to success was not a realistic one for them to follow. Instead, he emphasized the importance of staying in school and getting a good education. "I wanted to set them straight on the likelihood of them making it," he explained. "I broke it down to them by saying that they even had a better chance of being an NBA player than they did a rapper. I was, like, 'Keep it real—there are about communities in need, such as the Scholarship Fund, College Prep and Exposure, International Exposure, Professional Development, Scholar Support, and Community and Goodwill Programs.

"I'm an old-school person," Gloria said. "I believe that you work for what you want—you don't sit around and wait for someone to give it to you," she added. "But once you give them motivation, they need support."[2]

Gloria Carter (left) started the Shawn Carter Foundation with her son to help provide access to quality education to children from low-income backgrounds.

1. Quoted in Elysa Gardner, "Jay Z's 'Old-School' Mom Stresses Education, Work Ethic," *USA Today*, last updated March 19, 2014. www.usatoday.com/story/life/people/2014/03/12/jay-z-mom-discusses-shawn-carter-foundation/6253469/.

2. Quoted in Gardner, "Jay Z's 'Old-School' Mom Stresses Education, Work Ethic."

200 or more NBA players getting a check. There are only about 10 to 20 rappers that are in the game making money with album after album. Do the math and get your education.'"[78] JAY-Z even established scholarship programs to help kids from the inner city living in poverty attend college.

Supporting Barack Obama

As part of his effort to make an impact on the world, JAY-Z became a high-profile supporter of then-Senator Barack Obama during the 2008 presidential election campaign. He held free concerts to encourage people to register to vote, spoke at

JAY-Z helped campaign for Barack Obama before the 2008 presidential election. He also campaigned for Obama again in 2012, as shown in this photograph.

rallies, and went on a tour of swing states with the candidate. He described the historic significance of Obama's quest to become the first African American president of the United States at a campaign appearance in Philadelphia: "Rosa Parks sat so Martin Luther King could walk. Martin Luther King walked so Obama could run. Obama's running so we all can fly."[79]

At one campaign rally, Obama made a famous reference to the JAY-Z song "Dirt Off Your Shoulder." The candidate responded to criticism from then-Senator Hillary Clinton—his main rival for the Democratic nomination—with a gesture of brushing it off his shoulder. Columnist Maureen Dowd remarked that "it had to be the first time in history that a presidential candidate had a hip-hop moment."[80]

JAY-Z was thrilled when Obama won the presidency. "The joy and incredible sense of pride … and the sense of hope that it gave everybody in America that we're all now included in the American dream was priceless,"[81] he said.

Wedding Bells

By the time he threw his considerable influence behind the Obama campaign, JAY-Z had sold more than 30 million records, earned 4 Grammy Awards, launched his own record label and clothing line, discovered and promoted several popular new recording artists, and become a powerful business executive. In addition, for $40,000 a month, he also rented a 4,825-square-foot (448 sq m), luxury penthouse apartment at the Time Warner Center near Central Park in New York City.

JAY-Z and Beyoncé married in 2008, cementing their status as a power couple in the music world.

On April 4, 2008, the apartment served as the setting for a wedding ceremony when JAY-Z married his longtime girlfriend, the successful singer, businesswoman, and actress Beyoncé. This joyous affair was kept a secret and was small compared to other extravagant celebrity weddings. The couple chose to go without a maid of honor and best man while standing beside each other during their vows. During the reception, which lasted until nearly 5 a.m., "neither of them performed, but everyone danced to a lot of hip-hop and oldies, including Jackson 5 and Whitney Houston."[82] To many longtime fans, the marriage seemed to be the culmination of an almost unbelievable rags-to-riches story.

JAY-Z returned to perform with Mary J. Blige on their co-headlining *Heart of the City Tour* the next day. While onstage, Blige offered well wishes to the newlyweds, saying "Congratulations to my man Jay-Z and my girl B."[83]

The Blueprint 3

JAY-Z added to his string of top-selling albums with a third installment in the *Blueprint* series, which was released on September 8, 2009. "I like the challenge of making great music and putting it out," he stated. "You have to make it for yourself, but of course you want people to appreciate it. I'm not immune to that."[84] *The Blueprint 3* soared to number 1 on the Billboard 200 and sold 476,000 copies in the first week.

Initial reception of *The Blueprint 3* was generally positive. However, some critics scrutinized him for his success in the rap genre, pulling from a place most rappers have yet to reach:

> *Jay-Z has to contend with a dilemma that Tupac or Biggie never did—how to be hip-hop's first Hall of Fame workhorse, docu-menting life on top rather than on the rise. By all indications, he'll continue to make good but not great music, replicating the form of his finest records minus the electric charge. What more can Jay-Z say? Not so much, apparently. But he says it well.*[85]

After a rewarding release, despite some unfavorable reviews, JAY-Z launched *The Blueprint 3 Tour*. The tour, which kicked off in September 2009 and wrapped up in March 2010, featured opening acts J. Cole, Wale, N.E.R.D., Trey Songz, and Young Jeezy. All tour dates took place in the United States and Canada.

Even though JAY-Z seemed to have accomplished more than any other rap star, there were still ventures he wanted to explore and critics he wanted to prove wrong. The rapper still had more valuable rhymes and artistry to offer the music world. His fans would soon see his future endeavors prove that his retirement was an enormous fluke—and that as a rapper, he was here to stay.

Chapter Six

Growing as an Artist and Businessman

Upon entering a new decade, JAY-Z was at the top of his career and happily married to the love of his life. While having achieved so much already, he remained open-minded and welcomed new life experiences. These ambitious undertakings would see him grow not only as an artist, but also as a person.

Hope for Haiti

On January 12, 2010, Haiti was hit with a catastrophic earthquake that left more than 200,000 dead and 895,000 Haitians homeless. The estimated damage done by this earthquake was $14 billion. In an effort to put forth a helping hand, JAY-Z, along with Rihanna, Swizz Beatz, and U2's Bono and The Edge, released the charity track "Stranded (Haiti Mon Amour)." Proceeds from the song went toward Partners in Health, which is a nonprofit organization devoted to

JAY-Z performed with Rihanna and U2 during the Hope for Haiti Now: A Global Benefit for Earthquake Relief event.

providing a preferential health care option for those living in poverty.

In addition to releasing the song, the artists participated in Hope for Haiti Now: A Global Benefit for Earthquake Relief on January 22 to raise money for those impacted by the deadly earthquake. They performed the track during the telethon, which raised $61 million. Other artists, such as Dave Matthews, Neil Young, Justin Timberlake, Jennifer Hudson, Madonna, Beyoncé, Chris Martin, Sting, Christina Aguilera, and the Roots performed at the event as well.

Decoded

JAY-Z released his autobiography and memoir, *Decoded*, on November 16, 2010. The book contained a collection of lyrics from the rapper and his explanations on what inspired each line. He also shared stories from his childhood growing up in the Marcy Houses and his beginnings in the rap industry among artists such as The Notorious B.I.G. and Tupac Shakur. Opening up about their safety before their rap careers, JAY-Z commented: "They were both perfectly safe before they started rapping; they weren't being hunted by killers until they got into music. Biggie was on the streets before he started releasing music, but he never had squads of shooters (or the Feds) coming after him until he was famous."[1]

The rapper also reflected on current events, such as the devastation caused by Hurricane Katrina in 2005 and its connection to poverty in the African American communities affected:

I don't remember exactly where I was in August 2005, but at the end of that month I was mostly in front of the television, like most other people, transfixed and upset by the story of Hurricane Katrina. Most Americans were horrified by what was happening down there, but I think for black

Performing with Other Artists

In 2010, JAY-Z toured with both Eminem and U2. First, he joined Eminem for *The Home & Home Tour*. They performed together in September 2010 for four dates, two in Detroit, Michigan, at Comerica Park and two in New York City at Yankee Stadium. The two rappers originally announced the concerts after attending a baseball game between the Detroit Tigers and New York Yankees in May 2010, letting fans know they would be performing together at both stadiums later that year. Rapper B.o.B. opened for the duo on the tour.

people, we took it a little more personally. I've been to shantytowns in Angola that taught me that what we consider to be crushing poverty in the United States has nothing to do with what we have materially—even in the projects, we're rich compared to some people in other parts of the world. I met people in those shantytowns who lived in one room houses with no running water who had to pay a neighbor to get water to go to the bathroom. Those kids in Angola played ball on a court surrounded by open sewage, and while they knew it was bad, they didn't realize just how [problematic] it was. It was shocking. And I know there are parts of the world even worse off than that.[2]

JAY-Z is shown here with a copy of his autobiography, *Decoded*.

JAY-Z also offered up his opinions on Barack Obama and other stories about what it is like living as one of the world's most successful rappers.

1. Quoted in Jem Aswad, "Jay-Z's 'Decoded' Excerpts: The Best Bits," *Rolling Stone*, November 5, 2010. www.rollingstone.com/music/news/jay-zs-decoded-excerpts-the-best-bits-20101105.

2. JAY-Z, *Decoded*. New York, NY: Spiegel & Grau, 2011, p. 218.

The dates also featured guest performers, such as Memphis Bleek, Bridget Kelly, Young Jeezy, 50 Cent, D12, The Alchemist, Trick Trick, G-Unit, Drake, Beyoncé, Kanye West, Rihanna, Chris Martin, Swizz Beatz, Nicki Minaj, and J. Cole. One special moment during all four nights of the tour included JAY-Z paying tribute to The Notorious B.I.G. by performing the late rapper's hits "Juicy" and "One More Chance." Performing at the New York shows, JAY-Z also invited hip-hop pioneer Kool Herc onto the stage to offer the humble words, "We wouldn't be here without you."[86]

Following this touring stint, JAY-Z opened for U2 on 10 tour dates in Australia and New Zealand in November and December of 2010. The rapper provided support for the band during their *360° Tour*, which was the tour launched to promote their album *No Line on the Horizon*. Big name artists, such as the Black Eyed Peas, Snow Patrol, and Muse, came out to support them in other large cities on their tour.

Watch the Throne

After sharing the stage with many artists on tour, JAY-Z decided it was time to collaborate on an entire album with one of his fellow rappers and close friends—Kanye West. Previously, West had worked on production for a few of JAY-Z's albums. JAY-Z had also served as a featured artist on a few of West's songs, including "Never Let Me Down" from his debut album *The College Dropout* in 2004, "Diamonds from Sierra Leone (Remix)" from 2005's *Late Registration*, and "Monster" and "So Appalled" from 2010's *My Beautiful Dark Twisted Fantasy*.

During promotion of the *My Beautiful Dark Twisted Fantasy* album, two songs surfaced online featuring JAY-Z: a remix of West's song "Power" and "Monster," which also included guest spots from Rick Ross, Nicki Minaj, and indie rock group Bon Iver. After this, Kanye announced on Twitter in August 2010 that he and JAY-Z were going to release a five-song album; however, this project later ended up evolving into a full album with twelve tracks.

The album, titled *Watch the Throne,* was released on August 8, 2011, and spawned seven singles including "H. A. M.," "Otis," "Lift Off," "N****s in Paris," "Why I Love You," "Gotta Have It," and "No

Church in the Wild." Guest artists on the album included Beyoncé on "Lift Off," Mr Hudson on "Why I Love You," and Frank Ocean on "Made in America" and on "No Church in the Wild," along with The-Dream. On the track "Otis," JAY-Z and West also incorporated a sample of soul singer Otis Redding's "Try a Little Tenderness."

Most critics gave the album positive reviews. The A.V. Club wrote, "*Watch The Throne* was crafted in the heat and intensity of a very specific cultural moment, but Kanye and especially Jay-Z have the long view in mind. The album has the flash to dazzle and the substance to last."[87] The Pop & Hiss music blog, which is run by the *Los Angeles Times*, said, "The result is a … fiery, smart, if problematic, collaboration that showcases the pair's distinct lyrical skills, their way around a metaphor and an ability to execute both a grand narrative and the details that turn it into truth. Musically, the production is captivating."[88] The album resulted in success for both rappers, as it topped the Billboard 200 chart, was certified platinum in the United States, and earned them seven Grammy nominations.

Once the album was released, the pair decided to head out on a joint tour called the *Watch the Throne Tour*. As of 2018, it is the second highest grossing hip-hop concert tour in history, making $75.6 million off of 63 shows. The *Watch the Throne* tour ran from October 2011 to June 2012 in the United States and Europe.

Blue Ivy

Another big milestone occurred for JAY-Z in 2011. This was the announcement of his first child at the 2011 MTV Video Music Awards in August. At the end of Beyoncé's performance of her song "Love On Top," which is featured on her fourth solo album, 4, she dropped the microphone and ripped open her purple glitter suit coat to reveal a baby bump. The camera cut to a proud looking JAY-Z, who was being congratulated by his friend Kanye West.

After this huge statement was made, JAY-Z and Kanye West headed out on their *Watch the Throne* tour. During the middle of the tour, Beyoncé gave birth to their first daughter on January 7, 2012—Blue Ivy Carter. Several people have speculated the significance of the child's name. For example, some point to the JAY-Z lyrics: "My favor-

Blue Ivy Carter is shown here with her parents in 2018.

ite hue is Jay-Z blue,"[89] which appears in his rap verse of the Young Jeezy song "Go Crazy." He also released three *Blueprint* albums throughout his career. Beyoncé's favorite number is also four, which translates to "IV" in Roman numerals, pronounced as "Ivy." She hinted at a possible source of inspiration for their daughter's name by posting an excerpt from a 2005 Rebecca Solnit novel called *A Field Guide to Getting Lost* on Tumblr in June 2012:

The world is blue at its edges and in its depths. This blue is the light that got lost. Light at the blue end of the spectrum does not travel the whole distance from the sun to us. It disperses among the molecules of the air, it scatters in the water. Water is colorless, shallow water appears to be the color of whatever lies underneath it, but deep water is full of this scattered light, the purer the water the deeper the blue. The sky is blue for the same reason, but the blue at the horizon, the blue of the land that seems to be dissolving into the sky, is a deeper, dreamier, melancholy blue, the blue at the farthest reaches of the places where you see for miles, the blue of distance. This light does not touch us, does not travel the whole distance, the light that gets lost, gives us the beauty of the world, so much of which is in the color blue.[90]

Blue Ivy has been featured on a number of JAY-Z and Beyoncé's songs. She was first featured on JAY-Z's track "Glory," which he dedicated to Blue Ivy and released on his Life+Times blog on January 9, 2012. At only two days old, she is heard crying on the track, which details JAY-Z and Beyoncé's pregnancy struggles, including a miscarriage Beyoncé suffered before becoming pregnant with Blue Ivy. At two years old, Blue Ivy also appeared on Beyoncé's track "Blue" from her self-titled 2013 album. She is also featured in the music video for the song, which was filmed in Rio de Janeiro, Brazil. Blue Ivy also made a cameo in Beyoncé's "Formation" music video. On JAY-Z's album *4:44*, which was released on July 6, 2017, Blue Ivy is featured on one of the three bonus tracks titled "Blue's Freestyle/We Family." She is heard freestyling on the track with lines such as, "Never seen a ceiling in my whole life."[91] Another vocal cameo shows up on the "Mi Gente" remix, a new version of J Balvin and Willy William's "Mi Gente," which they released as a single with all the proceeds going to disaster victims in Puerto Rico, Mexico, and other Caribbean islands affected by Hurricane Maria in 2017.

Barclays Center

JAY-Z signed on as part owner of the Brooklyn Nets, formerly known as the New Jersey Nets, in 2004 after real estate developer Bruce Ratner purchased the team for $300 million in an effort to move the team from New Jersey to Brooklyn. Once the deal for the Brooklyn Nets' building was fully in place in 2010, construction of the multi-purpose indoor arena began. The arena, housed on Atlantic Avenue in Brooklyn, opened on September 21, 2012, and JAY-Z performed eight sold-out shows when it first opened. "I've been on many stages, been around the world, but nothing feels like tonight," JAY-Z told the crowd on the first night's performance. "Nothing feels like tonight, Brooklyn. I swear to God."[92]

Construction of this arena in Brooklyn meant a lot to JAY-Z since he had grown up 15 minutes away from where it was built, in the Marcy Houses. Witnessing significant growth in an area so close to his old neighborhood indicated progress not only for him, but also for people he grew up with and those currently living in the vicinity still struggling like he once had. He hoped the project would bring jobs and hope to those in the area.

For this series of performances, the rapper played a two-hour set, as he incorporated two decades worth of material. He opened the show with his 1997 track "Where I'm From," which was appropriate due to the celebratory circumstances. Originally, he had said no

Made In America Festival

In 2012, JAY-Z achieved another new feat by founding the Made in America Festival, an annual music festival held in Philadelphia, Pennsylvania, on Labor Day weekend. The music festival incorporates multiple music genres including hip-hop, indie rock, experimental rock, electronic dance music (EDM), alternative rock, R&B, pop, Latin, and more. As JAY-Z said, the whole concert is about displaying the diversity in America's music:

> *Through all the lines and things that are put in place to divide each other, all like-minded people gather together … We're more curious than ever. We create music to express ourselves. And when the world relates, ya know, that's beautiful things. We're all trading off each other's culture. So no matter what lines you put—country, indie rock, rap—we're all somehow gonna find a way to come together cause the lines and the titles can never keep us apart. This is what we've been. To put that on display for the world is, is just being honest. That's it, that's what it's all about. We are finally living out our creed.*[1]

A documentary about the festival titled *Jay-Z: Made in America*, directed by Ron Howard and produced by Brian Grazer and JAY-Z, was released on October 11, 2013. Howard said the documentary is "a reflection of the fabric of what it means to be 'Made in America'— what the festival represents, why Jay is doing it and how he relates to each artist."[2]

1. Quoted in Alvin Aqua Blanco, "Jay-Z x Budweiser—Makers of Tomorrow (Made In America Festival Commercial) [VIDEO]," HipHopWired, July 27, 2012. hiphopwired.com/174175/jay-z-x-budweiser-makers-of-tomorrow-made-in-america-festival-commercial-video/.

2. Quoted in CBS News, "Beyonce to Play Jay-Z's Made in America Festival," CBSNews, April 10, 2013. www.cbsnews.com/news/beyonce-to-play-jay-zs-made-in-america-festival/.

special guests would join him on stage, nevertheless Bedford-Stuyvesant rap legend Big Daddy Kane emerged during the encore to sing 1988's "Ain't No Half-Steppin'" and 1989's "Warm It Up, Kane."

As JAY-Z was about to wrap up the evening, he left the audience with the inspirational message that anyone has the potential to achieve their dreams if they put in the work and want it bad enough: "I ain't no different from anyone in this room, and now I'm standing on this stage, living proof."[93] The Barclays Center has since welcomed many artists to the stage, including Janet Jackson, Kendrick Lamar, Paul McCartney, Justin Bieber, and Katy Perry. The Barclays Center is also the home base of the New York Islanders hockey team.

Sports Projects

On top of being a partial owner of the Brooklyn Nets, JAY Z also served as an executive producer of the 2K Sports basketball video game *NBA2K13*. The game was released for multiple gaming systems, and the rapper had a prominent role in the making of the game. "Jay is so obsessed with authenticity," said Jason Argent, senior vice president at 2K Sports. "He really didn't want to just put his name on a product. Neither did we. We wanted a true collaboration with him."[94] Much of what he helped out with included the overall graphic flow of the game, as well as the intro and outro videos. He also curated the 24-song video game soundtrack, which included songs by the rapper himself, along with Santigold, Daft Punk, the Dirty Projectors, Nas, Meek Mill, and more. "It's much more music [and] cultural oriented," Argent said. "There are visuals of musicians and him interwoven with game play. It's really basketball within an entertainment and music package."[95]

Another sports venture JAY-Z took on in April 2013 was the launching of Roc Nation Sports, a management consulting, media, and entertainment company partnering with Creative Artists Agency (CAA) to represent athletes of different sports, such as baseball, American football, basketball, association football, and boxing. "Because of my love of sports, it was a natural progression to form a company where we can help top athletes in various sports the same way we have been helping artists in the music industry for years,"[96] JAY-Z said. The first athlete to sign on to JAY-Z's venture was Major League Baseball (MLB) player Robinson Cano, who played for the New York Yankees until signing with Seattle Mariners in December 2013. Other athletes signed to Roc Nation Sports include NBA player Kevin Durant, National Football League (NFL) player Dez Bryant, and Skylar Diggins-Smith of the Women's National Basketball Association (WNBA).

Magna Carta ... Holy Grail

In the midst of all these business deals, JAY-Z was planning for the release of his 12th studio album, *Magna Carta ... Holy Grail*. The announcement of his new album was made during a Samsung commercial played on June 16, 2013. Producers on the album include Rick Rubin, Pharrell Williams, Timbaland, and Swizz Beatz. "The album is about, like this duality of how do you navigate through this whole thing, through success, through failures, through all this and remain yourself," JAY-Z tells Rubin in the commercial. "We don't have any rules. Everyone's trying to figure it out ... We need to write the new rules."[97] For the release of the album, JAY-Z sold 1 million copies of the record to Samsung. Samsung then gave free copies of the album to the first 1 million users of the Samsung Galaxy S III, Galaxy S 4, and Galaxy Note II phones to download an application called Magna Carta, after the album, on July 4, 2013. The album was then released to the public on July 7, 2013.

The album, which topped the Billboard 200 chart, received mixed reviews from critics. Music reviewer Jordan Sargent from *Spin* wrote, "It's hard to view this piece of music—this art—through any prism besides the business one. The songs themselves—overwrought yet somehow still undercooked—don't do much to shift the perspective, either. This is a businessman making a business deal, with listeners simply left to handle the moving parts."[98] Randall Roberts of the *Los Angeles Times* had a slightly more positive review of the album: "'Magna Carta Holy Grail' certainly is shimmering, heavy and at times sonically stunning, and Jay-Z can toss a brilliant metaphor like it's nothing. But a true masterpiece harnesses intellect and adventure to push forward not only musically but also thematically. Which is to say, sure, call it a Picasso—but just don't compare it to 'Guernica

[Picasso's most famous work]."[99]

The first single released from *Magna Carta ... Holy Grail* on July 4, 2013, was "Holy Grail," which featured guest vocals from Justin Timberlake. The track peaked at number 4 on the Billboard Hot 100 chart. The video for the song also made history on August 29, 2013, as the first major music video to debut exclusively on Facebook. Additional songs released as singles from the album include "Tom Ford," which was the second single, and "Part II (On the Run)" featuring Beyoncé, which was the third single.

More Collaborations

In 2013, JAY-Z also did guest vocals on Justin Timberlake's song "Suit & Tie," a track from the pop singer's third solo album, *The 20/20 Experience*. The lead single from Timberlake's album was released on January 13, 2013. JAY-Z was featured in the music video for the track, which shows Timberlake and him dressed in suits while performing on stage. The song reached number 3 on the Billboard Hot 100 chart.

JAY-Z also appeared on Beyoncé's song "Drunk in Love" from her self-titled fifth solo album. The single debuted on December 13, 2013, and reached number 2 on the Billboard Hot 100 chart. In the black-and-white music video, Beyoncé and JAY-Z are seen dancing together on a beach at night.

As the husband and wife duo entered 2014, their sixth year of marriage, they were faced with some of their most difficult challenges, testing the strength of their relationship, their creativity, and willingness to grant forgiveness.

JAY-Z teamed up with Justin Timberlake in 2013 to guest rap on the latter's song "Suit & Tie," which was featured on *The 20/20 Experience*.

Chapter Seven

Family Matters

Approaching 2014, JAY-Z was ruling the rap world with nine Grammy nominations. He recently released his 12th studio album, *Magna Carta … Holy Grail*, and claimed ownership over several other successful business dealings. At the 56th Annual Grammy Awards in January 2014, he claimed the Best Rap/Sung Collaboration for "Holy Grail" from his album, *Magna Carta … Holy Grail,* and Best Music Video for Justin Timberlake's "Suit & Tie." Adding two more Grammys to his already hefty stack of awards, JAY-Z had not anticipated the drama that was to come next.

Elevator Controversy

JAY-Z found himself in the middle of a family altercation after the Met Gala on May 5, 2014. After attending the event with Beyoncé, they headed to The Standard Hotel in New York City for a Met Gala after-party with Beyoncé's sister Solange. While riding the elevator, Solange attacked JAY-Z, hitting and kicking him before being restrained by a security guard. At one point, Beyoncé intervened, trying to diffuse the situation. Unfortunately for all parties involved, the incident was caught on tape due to a video camera in the elevator. The surveillance footage of the attack was leaked by a hotel employee, who was later fired by the hotel for his actions, to the celebrity news website TMZ, who posted it for the public to see. A few days later the three recording artists released a joint statement:

> As a result of the public release of the elevator security footage from Monday, May 5th, there has been a great deal of speculation about what triggered the unfortunate incident. But the most important thing is that our family has worked through it …

> Jay and Solange each assume their share of responsibility for what has occurred. They both acknowledge their role in this private matter that has played out in the public. They both have apologized to each other and we have moved forward as a united family.

> The reports of Solange being intoxicated or displaying erratic behavior throughout that evening are simply false … At the end of the day families have problems and we're no different. We love each other and above all we are family. We've put this behind us and hope everyone else will do the same.[100]

Several speculations about what caused the incident came out—from cheating to break-up rumors for the married couple. However, an official reason for the occurrence has never been addressed. All three recording artists have cleverly made mention or alluded to the incident on their subsequent albums: JAY-Z's 4:44, Beyoncé's *Lemonade*, and Solange's *A Seat at the Table*. In the lyrics of JAY-Z's song "Kill Jay Z," the rapper references the event: "You egged Solange on, knowin' all along, all you had to say you was wrong."[101]

Launching TIDAL

JAY-Z took a leap in January 2015 by purchasing the Sweden-based company Aspiro for $56 million. Through this purchase, he constructed and launched TIDAL—the first artist-owned digital-music streaming service. On March 30, 2015, he threw a TIDAL launch

Supporting Hillary Clinton

Before the 2016 U.S. presidential election between Democratic candidate Hillary Clinton and Republican candidate Donald Trump, both JAY-Z and Beyoncé threw their support behind Clinton. The couple assisted Clinton in her campaign by making an appearance and performing at the Get Out the Vote event at the Wolstein Center in Cleveland, Ohio, on November 4, 2016. The event occurred a few days before Election Day, and other artists such as Chance The Rapper and Big Sean also appeared. Their efforts were meant to help increase the young black voter turnout.

Clinton had kind words to say about both JAY-Z and Beyoncé's contributions to society and mentioned some lyrics from JAY-Z's song, "My President is Black." She also expressed her appreciation for Beyoncé's lyrics and how she touches on some of the most important challenges America is currently facing, including poverty, racism, and the country's need for criminal justice reform.

Beyoncé and JAY-Z appeared at a Get Out the Vote event with Hillary Clinton in 2016.

party at New York City's James A. Farley Post Office in Herald Square. He was joined at the event by some of the biggest names in the music business, and each was offered a 3 percent stake in the company upon signing on as exclusive artists. As exclusive artists, they would release their new music first on TIDAL and offer up other special content to subscribers of the music streaming service. These artists included Beyoncé, Rihanna, Kanye West, Jack White, Arcade Fire, Usher, Nicki Minaj, Coldplay, Alicia Keys, Calvin Harris, Daft Punk, deadmau5, Jason Aldean, J. Cole, and Madonna. Each of these artists signed the TIDAL manifesto, which stated, "Tidal is an artist majority-owned company with a mission to reestablish the value of music and protect the sustainability of the music industry rooted in creativity and expression. ... Our movement is being led by a few who are inviting all to band together for a common cause, a movement to change the status quo."[102]

JAY-Z began TIDAL because he wanted to give some power back to the artists in the music industry while also bringing a higher quality product to consumers, especially people who respect and enjoy music. Alicia Keys explained the main goal of TIDAL at the event: "Our goal is simple: We want to create a better service and a better experience for both fans and artists ... We believe that it is in everyone's interests—fans, artists and the industry as a whole—to preserve the value of music, and to ensure a healthy and robust industry for years to come."[103]

In March 2016, TIDAL reported having 3 million subscribers; however, additional reports claimed that this estimate may have been inflated. According to *Forbes*, a month after these projections were released, the company's internal count stood at only 1.2 million. Later, a lawyer rejected all accusations concerning how many subscribers the music streaming service actually had. Despite these reports, TIDAL has managed to achieve considerable success with a 42 million-song catalog and availability in 52 countries. However, as of 2018, TIDAL falls below the amount of users that other music streaming services, such as Spotify and Apple Music, have. In January 2017, JAY-Z sold his stake in the company.

Lemonade *Released*

As one of the artist shareholders of TIDAL, Beyoncé released her sixth solo album, *Lemonade*, exclusively on the music streaming service on April 23, 2016. She released the 12-track album with no prior promotion of the actual album; however, she did release teaser clips of her HBO special titled *Lemonade*, which is the short film that debuted right before the surprise album was released.

TIDAL described the album as a "conceptual project based on every woman's journey of self-knowledge and healing."[104] The film presented thematic elements dealing with issues of race, misogyny, black womanhood, and marital unfaithfulness, the last of which sparked rumors of JAY-Z and Beyoncé's marriage potentially falling apart.

One particular line in Beyoncé's song "Sorry" that created controversy was, "He better call Becky with the good hair."[105] This line seems to point to a specific person, which many fans claim as someone who JAY-Z may have had romantic relations with during his marriage. However, Diana Gordon, one of the main songwriters for the track, was surprised at how much reaction and speculation came from fans regarding the song: "I laughed [at the reaction], like this is so silly. Where are we living? I was like, 'What day in age from that lyric do you get all of this information?' Is it really telling you all that much, accusing people?"[106] While Beyoncé never formally addressed the meaning behind the line, JAY-Z touched on these allegations in the title track from his 13th studio album, 4:44: "I apologize, often womanize/ Took for my child to be born/ See through a woman's eyes/ Took for these natural twins to believe in miracles/ Took me too long for this song/ I don't deserve you."[107]

Welcoming the Twins

The twins JAY-Z referred to are Rumi and Sir Carter, a daughter and a son he welcomed with Beyoncé on June 13, 2017, at Ronald Reagan UCLA Medical Center in Los Angeles. In an Instagram post on February 1, 2017, Beyoncé announced that her and JAY-Z were expecting two babies with a photo of herself cradling her baby bump with a sheer veil over her head while kneeling in front of a backdrop of colorful flowers. The caption for the photo read, "We would like to share our love and happiness. We have been blessed two times over … We are incredibly grateful that our family will be growing by two, and we thank you for your well wishes.—The Carters."[108] As for the announcement of the twins arrival, Beyoncé's father Mathew Knowles confirmed the news with a photo of balloons on Twitter with a message that read: "Happy Birthday to the twins! Love, Granddad."[109]

Songwriters Hall of Fame

JAY-Z was the first rapper to be inducted into the Songwriters Hall of Fame on June 15, 2017, at an event held at New York City's Marriot Marquis Hotel. However, the rapper was unable to attend the occasion due to Beyoncé's upcoming delivery of their twins in Los Angeles. Luckily, his mother and grandmother were in attendance to witness a video of President Barack Obama congratulating JAY-Z on receiving the honor. Obama said during the induction,

> I like to think Mr. Carter and I understand each other ... Nobody who met us as younger men would have expected us to be where we are today. We know what it's like not to have a father around. We know what it's like not to come from much, to know people didn't get the same breaks that we did, so we try to prop open those doors of opportunity so that it's a little easier for those who come up behind us to succeed as well.[1]

JAY-Z's acceptance speech was given by Jon Platt, CEO of Warner/Chappell Music Publishing, who said, "The hip-hop community has a very long history of being told you're not songwriters. This induction is a signal that your time has come and your time is now."[2] Other 2017 inductees included Robert Lamm and James Pankow, Kenneth "Babyface" Edmonds, Jimmy Jam and Terry Lewis, Berry Gordy, and Max Martin.

1. Quoted in Deena Zaru, "Obama Inducts Jay Z into Songwriters Hall of Fame and Reflects on Their Bond," CNN.com, August 14, 2017. www.cnn.com/2017/06/16/politics/obama-jay-z-songwriters-hall-of-fame/index.html.

2. Quoted in Melinda Newman, "Jay Z Becomes First Rapper Inducted Into Songwriters Hall Of Fame With Assist From Obama," Forbes, June 16, 2017. www.forbes.com/sites/melindanewman/2017/06/16/jay-z-becomes-first-rapper-inducted-into-songwriters-hall-of-fame-with-assist-from-obama/#72a812053c70.

It has been said they named their daughter Rumi "after a Persian poet, mystic and Islamic scholar called Rumi, born over 800 years ago—because he's his and Bey's [Beyoncé's] favourite."[110] Beyoncé released the first photo of the twins a month after they were born, and in the photo, she holds the two babies while standing in front of another display of flowers.

Release of 4:44

Once Beyoncé released *Lemonade*, which included accusations of JAY-Z's cheating, the public was wondering if these claims were true or just another publicity stunt to increase

Beyoncé performed while pregnant with twins at the 2017 Grammy Awards.

album sales. They also were waiting to hear JAY-Z's side of the story. Luckily, on June 30, 2017, JAY-Z released *4:44*, a collection of songs many regard as conscious hip-hop. The album also addressed the cheating rumors presented by *Lemonade*. Starting out, these two albums were meant to become a joint album; however, Beyoncé's music was further along than JAY-Z's, so she released her album first and JAY-Z's followed. This time, the pair made music together "almost like a therapy session," JAY-Z said. "I was right there the entire time."[111] During this creative process, JAY-Z and Beyoncé explored their relationship, which was in a rocky state due to the elevator video released by TMZ and rumors about cheating. However, instead of avoiding the issues in their relationship, they confronted them head on, and through their music, they expressed their emotions and found resolution. JAY-Z spoke on this challenge of facing the problems in their relationship: "The best place is right in the middle of the pain. And that's where we were sitting. And it was uncomfortable. And we had a lot of conversations. [I was] really proud of the music she made, and she was really proud of the art I released. And, you know, at the end of the day we really have a healthy respect for one another's craft. I think she's amazing."[112]

Throughout the title track on *4:44*, JAY-Z hints at his cheating behaviors and seems to apologize to his wife for his behavior: "I apologize to all the women whom I/ Toyed with your emotions 'cause I was emotionless/ And I apologize 'cause at your best you are love/ And because I fall short of what I say I'm all about/ Your eyes leave with the soul that your body once housed."[113] He also touches on another intimate detail of their relationship—the miscarriage Beyoncé suffered before they had their first child: "I seen the innocence leave your eyes/ I still mourn this death."[114] In the last verse of the song, he also speaks about his children and his past mistakes: "And if my children knew/ I don't even know what I would do/ If they ain't look at me the same/ I would prob'ly die with all the shame."[115]

In an exclusive *New York Times* interview with Dean Baquet, JAY-Z revealed he was unfaithful to Beyoncé and talked about coming to terms with what he had done. He also recognized that his difficult childhood partially caused him to isolate himself and make bad decisions directly linked to emotions and relationships: "You have to survive. So you go into survival mode, and when you go into survival mode, what happens? You shut down all emotions. So even with women, you gonna shut down emotionally, so you can't connect … In my case, like, it's deep. And then all the things happen from there: infidelity."[116]

JAY-Z was nominated for eight Grammys at the 60th annual Grammy Awards, which took place on January 28, 2018 at Madison Square Garden in New York City. The album *4:44* was nominated for Album of the Year and Best Rap Album. The song "4:44" was nominated for Song of the Year and Best Rap Performance, while "The Story of O.J." was nominated for Best Rap Song, Record of the Year, and Best Music Video. His song "Family Feud," which features Beyoncé, was nominated for Best Rap/ Sung Collaboration.

4:44 Tour

Once JAY-Z released *4:44*, he took a few months before going out on tour so he could spend time with the twins, Rumi and Sir, who arrived in June slightly before the release of his album. The tour began on October 27, 2017, at the Honda Center in

Anaheim, California, and ended on December 21, 2017, at The Forum in Inglewood, California. Vic Mensa served as the opener on the tour, which made stops in the United States and Canada.

JAY-Z included his entire career of hit songs on this tour, which featured some of his new tracks, such as "Kill Jay Z," "4:44," and "Smile," along with some old favorites, such as "Hard Knock Life (Ghetto Anthem)," "Empire State of Mind," "Run This Town," "On to the Next One," "Dirt off Your Shoulder," and "Izzo (H.O.V.A.)." The tour grossed more than $44 million.

JAY-Z performed hit songs, which spanned his entire career, during his *4:44 Tour.*

"Smile"

Another pivotal moment in JAY-Z's life in 2017 was when his mother Gloria Carter revealed to him that she was a lesbian. She waited years to reveal this and kept it a secret from her four children as she raised them and even into their adulthood. However, one day, she decided it was time to tell JAY-Z about this part of her identity: "I just finally started telling him who I was … Besides your mother, this is the person that I am. This is the life that I live. So my son actually started tearing, because he was like, 'That had to be a horrible life, Ma.' And I was like, 'My life was never horrible, it was just different.'"[117]

After hearing his mother's confession, he was inspired to include her harrowing journey of self-discovery and courage to open up about it on his album *4:44*. The third track, titled "Smile," includes the lyrics: "Mama had four kids, but she's a lesbian/ Had to pretend so long that she's a thespian/ Had to hide in the closet, so she medicate/ Society shame and the pain was too much to take/ Cried tears of joy when you fell in love/ Don't matter to me if it's a him or her/ I just wanna see you smile through all the hate."[118] His mother is also featured on the track reciting "Living in the Shadows," a poem she wrote during a plane trip on her way to see her son.

The reason she kept this part of herself a secret for such a long time was not to protect herself, but to ward off any rumors about her dating life that might have affected other women and families due to her status as JAY-Z's mother. Now that she has expressed her true self to her son and the rest of world, she feels much more liberated:

> *I was never ashamed of me, but my family, it was something that was never discussed ... Because everybody knows who I am, I don't hide who I am ... I'm tired of all the mystery. I'm gonna give it to 'em. I don't have to worry about anybody wondering whether I'm in the life or not—I'm gonna tell them. Now it's time for me to ... live my life and be happy, be free.*[119]

Future of a Famous Rapper

Over the years, JAY-Z has shown no signs of relinquishing his spot at the top of the music industry. Insiders routinely marvel that one of the most impressive things about JAY-Z has been his staying power. Unlike many previous rap stars, he has remained tremendously popular for many years. "We've seen rappers killed, or just fall off," L. A. Reid said. "Now we're watching the biggest rapper remain the biggest rapper. We've never seen this movie before."[120]

Given his many accomplishments and his lasting influence on hip-hop culture, it is little wonder that numerous sources have referred to JAY-Z as the greatest MC of all time. JAY-Z declined to compare himself to top artists of the past, but he expressed determination to be the best that he could possibly be. "I can't get into that argument," he said, "because the people at the top of the game are no longer here with us. Big [The Notorious B.I.G.] and 'Pac [Tupac Shakur] didn't really get a chance to grow as artists. We never got to see where it woulda went. But I always felt that's what I was comin' to do, to be the best. I wasn't comin' in the game to be nothin' less."[121]

Notes

Introduction: Rise to the Top

1. Touré, "Jay-Z: The Black Album," *Rolling Stone*, November 19, 2003. www.rollingstone.com/music/albumreviews/the-black-album-20031119.

2. Quoted in Josh Tyrangiel, "In His Next Lifetime," *TIME*, November 17, 2003. content.time.com/time/magazine/article/0,9171,543787,00.html.

3. Jake Brown, *JAY-Z … and the Roc-A-Fella Records Dynasty*. Phoenix, AZ: Colossus Books, 2005, p. 227.

4. Brown, *JAY-Z … and the Roc-A-Fella Records Dynasty*, p. xv.

5. Russell Simmons, "Jay-Z," *TIME*, April 18, 2005. content.time.com/time/specials/packages/article/0,28804,1972656_1972707_1973531,00.html.

Chapter One: Finding His Way

6. Quoted in Brown, *Jay-Z … and the Roc-A-Fella Records Dynasty*, p. 9.

7. David Kohn, "The King of Rap," *60 Minutes*, November 18, 2002. www.cbsnews.com/stories/2002/11/18/60II/main529811.shtml.

8. Quoted in Brown, *Jay-Z … and the Roc-A-Fella Records Dynasty*, p. 13.

9. Quoted in Emma Forrest, "JAY-Z: Hip-Hop's Hottest Guy Talks about It All," *Teen People*, June 16, 2002, p. 54.

10. Quoted in Brown, *JAY-Z … and the Roc-A-Fella Records Dynasty*, pp. 6–7.

11. Quoted in Lorraine Ali, "The Coolest Mogul," *Newsweek*, December 3, 2006. www.newsweek.com/coolest-mogul-105165.

12. Quoted in Brown, *JAY-Z … and the Roc-A-Fella Records Dynasty*, p. 7.

13. Quoted in Touré, "The Book of Jay," *Rolling Stone*, December 15, 2005. www.rollingstone.com/music/features/the-book-of-jay-20051215.

14. Quoted in Touré, "The Book of Jay."

15. Quoted in Kohn, "The King of Rap."

16. Quoted in Kohn, "The King of Rap."

17. Quoted in Dennis Abrams, *Jay-Z (Hip-Hop Stars)*. New York, NY: Chelsea House, 2012, p. 41.

18. Quoted in Touré, "The Book of Jay."

19. Quoted in Touré, "The Book of Jay."

20. Steve Huey, "Jay-Z *Reasonable Doubt*," AllMusic, accessed January 24, 2018. www.allmusic.com/album/reasonable-doubt-mw0000181538.

21. Quoted in Kris Ex, "Jayhova's Witness," *Vibe*, December 2000, p. 134.

Chapter Two: Moving Up the Rap Ladder

22. Quoted in Simon Vozick-Levinson, "The Real Return of the King," *Entertainment Weekly*, October 26, 2007. ew.com/music/2007/10/26/jay-zs-american-gangster-real-deal/.

23. Quoted in "Jay-Z Interview on Centerstage part 3," YouTube video, 7:41, posted by Basketballjordanpip, February 17, 2010. www.youtube.com/watch?v=SGQUnSJ9Ao8.

24. Quoted in Nick Charles and Cynthia Wang, "Street Singer," *People*, April 5, 1999. people.com/archive/street-singer-vol-51-no-12/.

25. Steven Thomas Erlewine, "Jay-Z Vol. 2 … Hard Knock Life," AllMusic, accessed January 24, 2018. www.allmusic.com/cg/amg.dll?p=amg&sql=10:jg3gtq9zmu46.

26. Bob Waliszewski, "Jay-Z: Vol. 2 … Hard Knock Life," Focus On The Family's Pluggedin. www.pluggedin.com/music-reviews/album/jayz-vol2hardknocklife/.

27. Quoted in Robert Brunner, "Cash of the Titans," *Entertainment Weekly*, May 30, 2003. ew.com/

article/2003/05/30/cash-titans/.

28. Quoted in Brunner, "Cash of the Titans."

29. Quoted in Forrest, "JAY-Z," p. 54.

30. Kris Ex, "Jay-Z: Vol. 3 Life and Times of S. Carter," *Rolling Stone*, February 3, 2000. www.rollingstone.com/music/albumreviews/vol-3-life-and-times-of-s-carter-20000203.

31. Quoted in Steve Jones, "Amid Hard Knocks, the Real Deal: Back for Another Round, JAY-Z Pulls No Punches," *USA Today*, December 27, 1999, p. D1.

32. Quoted in Lauren DeCarlo, "JAY-Z Goes on the Record," WWD, September 15, 2005, p. 20.

33. Quoted in Brunner, "Cash of the Titans."

34. Quoted in Forrest, "JAY-Z," p. 54.

35. Quoted in Tyrangiel, "In His Next Lifetime."

Chapter Three: Rap Retirement

36. Jason Birchmeier, "Jay-Z The Blueprint," AllMusic, accessed January 24, 2018. www.allmusic.com/cg/amg.dll?p=amg&sql=10:wxfrxq80ldde.

37. Neil Strauss, "The Blueprint: JAY-Z," *Rolling Stone*, October 2, 2001. www.rollingstone.com/music/albumreviews/the-blueprint-20011002.

38. Quoted in Touré, "People of the Year 2001: Jay-Z," *Rolling Stone*, p. 131.

39. Christian Hoard, "Jay-Z: The Blueprint, Vol. 2: The Gift and the Curse,"*Rolling Stone*, November 12, 2002. www.rollingstone.com/music/albumreviews/the-blueprint-vol-2-the-gift-and-the-curse-20021112.

40. Quoted in Tyrangiel, "In His Next Lifetime."

41. Quoted in Tyrangiel, "In His Next Lifetime."

42. Touré, "JAY-Z: The Black Album."

43. Quoted in Brian B., "Jay-Z Talks About His New Film Fade to Black," MovieWeb, November 4, 2004. movieweb.com/jay-z-talks-about-his-new-film-fade-to-black/.

44. Quoted in Steve Jones, "The Show Goes On for Jay-Z," *USA Today*, November 5, 2004, p. E12.

Chapter Four: Building a Business Empire

45. Jeff Leeds and Lola Ogunnaike, "'Retired' Rapper Finds a Job Atop Def Jam," *New York Times*, December 9, 2004. www.nytimes.com/2004/12/09/business/media/retired-rapper-finds-a-job-atop-def-jam.html.

46. Quoted in Allison Samuels, "The Reign of JAY-Z," *Newsweek*, November 21, 2004. www.newsweek.com/reign-jay-z-124335.

47. Quoted in Samuels, "The Reign of JAY-Z."

48. Quoted in Samuels, "The Reign of JAY-Z."

49. Quoted in Samuels, "The Reign of JAY-Z."

50. Quoted in Jones, "The Show Goes on for JAY-Z," p. E12.

51. Quoted in Nadira A. Hira, "America's Hippest CEO," *Fortune*, October 17, 2005. archive.fortune.com/magazines/fortune/fortune_archive/2005/10/17/8358069/index.htm.

52. Quoted in Tamara Conniff, "JAY-Z Named President, CEO of Def Jam Records," *Billboard*, December 8, 2004. www.billboard.com/articles/news/65356/jay-z-named-def-jam-presidentceo.

53. Quoted in Touré, "The Book of Jay."

54. Quoted in Ali, "The Coolest Mogul."

55. Quoted in Samuels, "The Reign of JAY-Z."

56. Quoted in Leeds and Ogunnaike, "'Retired' Rapper Finds a Job Atop Def Jam."

57. Quoted in Touré, "The Book of Jay."

58. Quoted in Steve Jones, "Jay-Z Is a Very Busy Man," *USA Today*, November 21, 2006, p. D5.

59. Quoted in Hira, "America's Hippest CEO."

60. Hira, "America's Hippest CEO."

61. Quoted in Jones, "Jay-Z Is a Very Busy Man," p. D5.

62. Quoted in Ali, The Coolest Mogul."

Chapter Five: The Comeback

63. Quoted in Gina Serpe, "Jay-Z Officially Unretires," *Eonline*, September 14, 2006. www.eonline.com/news/53319/jay-z-officially-unretires.

64. Quoted in Vozick-Levinson, "The Real Return of the King."

65. Rob Sheffield, "Jay-Z: American Gangster," *Rolling Stone*, November 15, 2007. www.rollingstone.com/music/album-reviews/american-gangster-20071115.

66. Quoted in Steve Jones, "For Jay-Z, Gangster Is the Soundtrack of His Life," *USA Today*, November 6, 2007, p. D1.

67. Quoted in Steve Jones, "Album, Film Round Out Jay-Z's Gangster Story," *USA Today*, November 6, 2007, p. D6.

68. Vozick-Levinson, "The Real Return of the King."

69. Quoted in Jones, "For Jay-Z, Gangster Is the Soundtrack of His Life," p. D1.

70. Sheffield, "American Gangster."

71. Quoted in Elliott Wilson, "The Audacity of Hov," *Vibe*, August 21, 2008, p. 128.

72. Quoted in Brunner, "Cash of the Titans."

73. Quoted in Jeff Leeds, "In Rapper's $150 Million Deal, New Model for Ailing Business," *New York Times*, April 3, 2008. query.nytimes.com/gst/fullpage.html?res=9A0CE4DF1E31 F930A35757C0A96E9C8B63.

74. Quoted in Abrams, *Jay-Z (Hip-Hop Stars)*, pp. 76–77.

75. Quoted in Samuels, "The Reign of JAY-Z."

76. Quoted in Nick Wadhams, "JAY-Z Helps U.N. Focus on Water Crisis," *Washington Post*, August 9, 2006. www.washingtonpost.com/wp-dyn/content/article/2006/08/09/AR2006080901311.html.

77. Quoted in Ali, "The Coolest Mogul."

78. Quoted in Samuels, "The Reign of JAY-Z."

79. Quoted in Dan Martin, "Jay-Z: Obama's Running So We All Can Fly," *The Guardian*, November 5, 2008. www.theguardian.com/music/2008/nov/05/jayz-falloutboy.

80. Maureen Dowd, "Brush It Off," *New York Times*, April 20, 2008. www.nytimes.com/2008/04/20/opinion/20dowd.html.

81. "Why Jay-Z Backed Barack," MTV News video, 1:33, posted January 19, 2009. www.mtv.com/video-clips/dgsr18/why-jay-z-backed-barack.

82. Quoted in Michelle Tauber, "Beyoncé and Jay-Z Married!" *People*, April 21, 2008. people.com/archive/cover-story-beyonce-and-jay-z-married-vol-69-no-15/.

83. Quoted in Tauber, "Beyoncé and Jay-Z Married!"

84. Quoted in Vozick-Levinson, "The Real Return of the King."

85. Jody Rosen, "Jay-Z: The Blueprint 3," *Rolling Stone*, September 14, 2009. www.rollingstone.com/music/album-reviews/the-blueprint-3-20090914.

Chapter Six: Growing as an Artist and Businessman

86. Quoted in Jason Gregory, "Jay-Z and Eminem Bring Kanye West, 50 Cent to Final New York Gig," Gigwise, September 15, 2010. www.gigwise.com/news/58419/jay-z-and-eminem-bring-kanye-west-50-cent-to-final-new-york-gig.

87. Nathan Rabin, "Kanye West and Jay-Z: Watch The Throne," The A.V. Club, August 9, 2011. music.avclub.com/kanye-west-and-jay-z-watch-the-throne-1798169205.

88. "Album Review: Jay-Z and Kanye West's 'Watch the Throne'," *Los Angeles Times*, August 8, 2011. latimesblogs.latimes.com/music_blog/2011/08/album-review-jay-z-and-kanye-wests-watch-the-throne.html.

89. Quoted in Ariana Finlayson, "Beyonce Hints at What Inspired Blue Ivy's Name," *Us Weekly*, June 14, 2012. www.usmagazine.com/celebrity-moms/news/beyonce-hints-at-what-inspired-blue-ivys-name-2012146/.

90. Quoted in Finlayson, "Beyonce Hints at What Inspired Blue Ivy's Name."

91. Quoted in Max Weinstein, "Blue Ivy is Rapping on JAY-Z's '4:44' Bonus Track," XXLmag, July 6, 2017. www.xxlmag.com/news/2017/07/blue-ivy-rapping-jay-z-444-bonus-track/.

92. Quoted in Simon Vozick-Levinson, "Jay-Z Represents Brooklyn at First Barclays Center Show," *Rolling Stone*, September 29, 2012. www.rollingstone.com/music/news/jay-z-represents-brooklyn-at-first-barclays-center-show-20120929.

93. Quoted in Vozick-Levinson, "Jay-Z Represents Brooklyn at First Barclays Center Show."

94. Quoted in Adam B. Vary, "Jay-Z Exec Producing Videogame 'NBA 2K13,' But What does That Mean?" *Entertainment Weekly*, July 31, 2012. ew.com/article/2012/07/31/jay-z-nba-2k13-tracklist/.

95. Quoted in Vary, "Jay-Z Exec Producing Videogame 'NBA 2K13,' But What does That Mean?"

96. Quoted in Justin Kroll, "Jay-Z Launches Roc Nation Sports Teams With CAA to Co-Represent Robinson Cano," *Variety*, April 2, 2013. variety.com/2013/biz/news/roc-nation-launches-roc-nation-sports-teams-with-caa-to-co-represent-robinson-cano-1200331923/.

97. Quoted in Erika Ramirez, "Jay-Z Announces New Album, 'Magna Carta Holy Grail,' in Samsung Commercial," *Billboard*, June 16, 2013. www.billboard.com/articles/columns/the-juice/1567101/jay-z-announces-new-album-magna-carta-holy-grail-in-samsung.

98. Jordan Sargent, "Review: Jay-Z, 'Magna Carta Holy Grail,'" *Spin*, July 5, 2013. www.spin.com/2013/07/jay-z-magna-carta-holy-grail-samsung-july-4/.

99. Randall Roberts, "Review: Jay-Z's 'Magna Carta Holy Grail' Full of Empty Boasts," *Los Angeles Times*, July 5, 2013. beta.latimes.com/entertainment/music/posts/la-et-ms-jay-z-review-20130705-story.html.

Chapter Seven: Family Matters

100. Quoted in Associated Press, "Beyoncé, Jay Z and Solange Break Silence About Video Drama," *People*, May 15, 2014. people.com/celebrity/beyonc-jay-z-and-solange-break-silence-about-video-drama/.

101. JAY-Z, "Kill Jay Z," Roc Nation. Originally released June 30, 2017.

102. Quoted in Todd Spangler, "Jay Z Launches Tidal Streaming-Music Service at Star-Studded Event," *Variety*, March 30, 2015. variety.com/2015/digital/news/jay-z-launches-tidal-streaming-music-service-1201462769/.

103. Quoted in Spangler, "Jay Z Launches Tidal Streaming-Music Service at Star-Studded Event."

104. Quoted in Brittany Spanos, "Beyonce Releases New Album 'Lemonade' on Tidal," *Rolling Stone*, April 23, 2016. www.rollingstone.com/music/news/beyonce-releases-new-album-lemonade-on-tidal-20160423.

105. Beyoncé, "Sorry," Parkwood. Originally released May 3, 2016.

106. Quoted in Jack Shepherd, "Beyoncé Writer Addresses 'Becky with the Good Hair' Lyric in 'Sorry,'" *Independent*, August 3, 2016. www.independent.co.uk/arts-entertainment/music/news/beyonce-diana-gordon-who-is-becky-meaning-sorry-a7169786.html.

107. JAY-Z, "4:44," Roc Nation. Originally released July 11, 2017.

108. Quoted in Char Adams and Lindsay Kimble, "Beyoncé Expecting Twins with Husband Jay Z: 'We Have Been Blessed Two Times Over,'" *People*, February 1, 2017. people.com/babies/beyonce-expecting-twins-pregnant-jay-z/.

109. Quoted in Melody Chiu and Jen Juneau, "Beyoncé and Jay Z 'Thrilled' to Welcome Twins as 'Granddad' Mathew Knowles Confirms News," *People*, June 17, 2017. people.com/babies/beyonce-jay-z-welcome-twins/.

110. Quoted in Olivia Waring, "Jay-Z Reveals the Inspiration Behind Their Kids' Names," PageSix.com, August 26, 2017. pagesix.com/2017/08/26/jay-z-reveals-the-inspiration-behind-their-kids-names/.

111. Quoted in Dean Baquet, "JAY-Z & Dean Baquet," *New York Times*, November 29, 2017. www.nytimes.com/interactive/2017/11/29/t-magazine/jay-z-dean-baquet-interview.html.

112. Quoted in Baquet, "JAY-Z & Dean Baquet."

113. JAY-Z, "4:44."

114. JAY-Z, "4:44."

115. JAY-Z, "4:44."

116. Quoted in Baquet, "JAY-Z & Dean Baquet."

117. Quoted in Jon Blistein, "Hear Jay-Z's Mother Reveal Why She Came Out on '4:44' Song," *Rolling Stone*, September 7, 2017. www.rollingstone.com/music/news/hear-jay-zs-mother-reveal-why-she-came-out-on-444-song-w501639.

118. JAY-Z, "Smile," Roc Nation. Originally released January 25, 2018.

119. Quoted in Blistein, "Hear Jay-Z's Mother Reveal Why She Came Out on '4:44' Song."

120. Quoted in Ali, "The Coolest Mogul."

121. Quoted in Brown, *JAY-Z … and the Roc-A-Fella Records Dynasty*, p. 132.

JAY-Z Year by Year

1969

JAY-Z is born with the name Shawn Corey Carter on December 4 in Brooklyn, New York.

1981

JAY-Z's father, Adnis Reeves, deserts the family; JAY-Z begins selling drugs on the streets.

1989

JAY-Z contributes vocals to "Hawaiian Sophie" by Jaz-O. The song becomes a minor hit, and JAY-Z gains recognition as a talented young rapper.

1995

JAY-Z forms Roc-A-Fella Records with partners Damon Dash and Kareem "Biggs" Burke.

1996

JAY-Z releases his first album, *Reasonable Doubt*, in June.

1997

Roc-A-Fella signs a joint venture agreement with Def Jam Records; JAY-Z releases second album, *In My Lifetime: Volume 1* in November.

1998

JAY-Z becomes a star with the release of his hugely successful third album, *Volume 2 … Hard Knock Life* in September.

1999

Following the release of *Volume 3 … Life and Times of S. Carter*, JAY-Z is arrested and charged with assault in connection with the stabbing of Lance "Un" Rivera at a New York nightclub in December.

2001

JAY-Z releases his critically acclaimed album *The Blueprint* in September.

2002

JAY-Z releases *The Blueprint 2* in November.

2003

JAY-Z announces his intention to retire as a recording artist to concentrate on business interests; JAY-Z releases *The Black Album* and holds a farewell concert at Madison Square Garden in November.

2005

JAY-Z accepts a job as president and CEO of Def Jam Records.

2006

JAY-Z ends his retirement and returns to recording with the album *Kingdom Come* in November.

2007

Inspired by the film of the same name, JAY-Z releases the concept album *American Gangster* in November; JAY-Z steps down as president of Def Jam.

2008

JAY-Z marries his longtime girlfriend, Beyoncé, in April; JAY-Z signs a $150 million deal with concert promoter Live Nation.

2009

JAY-Z releases *The Blueprint 3*.

2010

JAY-Z releases charity track "Stranded (Haiti Mon Amour)" to benefit victims of the deadly earthquake in Haiti; he performs at Hope for Haiti Now: A Global Benefit for Earthquake Relief in January; he tours with Eminem in Detroit and New York City in September and tours with U2 in Australia and New Zealand in November and December; and he releases his autobiography, *Decoded*, in December.

2011

JAY-Z and Kanye West release their collaboration album, *Watch the Throne*, in August; Beyoncé announces she and her husband are expecting their first child at the MTV Video Music Awards in August; and JAY-Z launches *Watch the Throne Tour* in October.

2012

Blue Ivy Carter is born on January 7; JAY-Z releases the track "Glory," which features Blue Ivy's voice, in January; Barclays Center opens in September; and JAY-Z founds the Made in America festival and kicks off the first year of the festival in September.

2013

JAY-Z raps on Justin Timberlake's single "Suit & Tie" in January; he launches Roc Nation Sports in April; he releases the album *Magna Carta ... Holy Grail* in July; and the *Jay-Z: Made in America* documentary is released in October.

2014

JAY-Z wins Best Rap/Sung Collaboration Grammy for "Holy Grail" in January; JAY-Z has an altercation with Solange and Beyoncé after the Met Gala in an elevator at The Standard Hotel in New York City in May.

2015

JAY-Z launches music streaming service TIDAL in March.

2016

JAY-Z campaigns for Democratic presidential candidate Hillary Clinton by performing at the Get Out the Vote event at the Wolstein Center in Cleveland, Ohio, in November.

2017

JAY-Z welcomes his second and third children, twins Rumi and Sir, with Beyoncé on June 13; JAY-Z becomes first rapper inducted into the Songwriters Hall of Fame; he releases his album *4:44* in June; he kicks off the *4:44 Tour* in October; and his mother, Gloria Carter, comes out as a lesbian.

For More Information

Books

Beaumont, Mark. *Jay Z: The King of America*. London, UK: Music Sales, 2012.
This biography of JAY-Z covers events from his early life, including his father abandoning him, his accidental shooting of his brother, and his experience dealing drugs.

Bulingame, Jeff. *Jay-Z: A Biography of a Hip-Hop Icon*. Berkeley Heights, NJ: Enslow Publishers, 2014.
Burlingame's biography examines JAY-Z's childhood, his rise to stardom as a rapper, his business deals, and his family life.

Dettmar, Kevin, and Jonathan Lethem, eds. *Shake It Up: Great American Writing on Rock and Pop from Elvis to Jay Z*. New York, NY: Library of America, 2017.
This book takes an in-depth look at rock and pop, as well as other musical genres. Some artists profiled in this book include Elvis Presley, Janis Joplin, and JAY-Z.

Greenburg, Zack O'Malley. *Empire State of Mind: How Jay-Z Went from Street Corner to Corner Office*. New York, NY: Portfolio/ Penguin, 2015.
This book explores the life of JAY-Z, from living in the Marcy Houses in Brooklyn to becoming one of the greatest MCs and most successful businessmen of all time.

Gunderson, Jessica. *Jay-Z: Hip-Hop Icon*. Mankato, MN: Capstone Press, 2012.
This graphic novel delves into JAY-Z's music career and life as a businessman in the music industry.

Websites

Google—Interactive History of Hip-Hop
(www.google.com/logos/2017/hiphop/hiphop17.html)
This Google website is an interactive DJ experience, which provides insight into the history and pioneers of hip-hop music.

JAY-Z on Facebook
(www.facebook.com/JayZ/)
JAY-Z connects with fans and notifies them of upcoming tour
dates, events, and new music on his official Facebook page.

JAY-Z on Twitter
(twitter.com/s_c_)
JAY-Z's official Twitter page is where he connects with his fans
through social media. He gives updates on tour information,
appearances, music news, and other life events.

JAY-Z: *Rolling Stone*
(www.rollingstone.com/music/artists/jay-z)
This section of the *Rolling Stone* website provides all the articles
it has published that make mention of JAY-Z.

Roc Nation Official Website: JAY-Z
(rocnation.com/jay-z/)
The official website for JAY-Z's record label, Roc Nation, includes
a biography on the rapper, his discography, links to his social
media profiles, and the artist's latest news.

Index

Picture Credits

Cover JStone/Shuttertstock.com; p. 7 Tinseltown/Shutterstock.com; p. 8 Theo Wargo/Getty Images; p. 10 Raymond Boyd/Getty Images; p. 17 Ray Tamarra/Getty Images; pp. 18, 37, 42 Johnny Nunez/WireImage/Getty Images; p. 27 David Corio/Michael Ochs Archives/Getty Images; p. 29 FeatureFlash Photo Agency/Shutterstock.com; p. 36 KMazur/WireImage/Getty Images; p. 39 Frank Micelotta/Getty Images; p. 41 TIMOTHY A. CLARY/AFP/Getty Images; p. 46 Everett Collection/Shutterstock.com; p. 52 Scott Gries/Getty Images; p. 57 Yui Mok - PA Images/PA Images via Getty Images; p. 59 Mike Coppola/WireImage/Getty Images; p. 60 LO Kin-hei/Shutterstock.com; p. 61 Kevin Mazur/WireImage/Getty Images; p. 63 Philip Ramey/Corbis via Getty Images; p. 65 Eugene Gologursky/WireImage/Getty Images; p. 68 Kevin Mazur/Getty Images for NARAS; p. 73 Lester Cohen/WireImage/Getty Images; p. 76 Brooks Kraft/Getty Images; p. 80 VALERIE MACON/AFP/Getty Images; p. 82 Kevin Mazur/Getty Images for Roc Nation.

About the Author

Vanessa Oswald is an experienced freelance writer and editor who has written pieces for publications based in New York City and the Western New York area, which include *Resource* magazine, *The Public*, *Auxiliary* magazine, and *Niagara Gazette*. In her spare time, she enjoys dancing, traveling, reading, snowboarding, and attending many live concerts.